Walnuts On My Bookshelf

Memories of Living in Communist Russia, 1952-1991

by

Peter Kirchikov

God Bless!

Peter Kirchikov.

Dedication

To my parents
Anna Petrovna Kirchikova and Kharlampyi Demyanovich Kirchikov

And to my sister and brother
Anna Kharlampyievna Kirchikova
&
Demyan Kirchikov

To whom I am so much indebted
and who mean everything to me.

Picture on the cover: left to right
Back row- standing: my sister, Peter Kirchikov
Front row: sitting: my dad, my nephew, my oldest son, my mother

Printed by Rocky Heights Print and Binding
206 Oak Mountain Circle
Pelham, AL 35124

Disclaimer: This book, writings, its digital version, ebook, script/written, electronic pieces and electronic/digital version are for information purposes only and do not imply or provide any type of advice: legal, computer, forensic, financial, etc. I am not an attorney and I am prohibited by state and federal laws from giving legal or any other type of advice. You should contact a legal practitioner for your specific needs. Views and opinions expressed in this selection, book, release, article, piece, script, electronic piece and electronic/digital versions and presentations are solely mine and do not reflect views, opinions and policies of any of my employers -- past, present or future -- or any other entity. Any references to companies, corporations, trademarks, registered marks, service marks, laws, law cites, names, entities, websites, etc. are for information purposes only and do not constitute any endorsements, approval or disapproval. I am not paid to promote anyone's products, services, or items. Any coincidences in this book with actual names, dates, events, biographies, characters, etc. and et al are incidental and neither intentional nor purposeful. Some of the actual names were replaced with assumed names. Peter Kirchikov.

Table of Contents

ACKNOWLEDGMENTS

I would like to extend my deepest gratitude to my wife, Carla, who inspired and encouraged me so much to write this book and offered so many brilliant ideas, topics, and suggestions. She is very special to me and my children, Ilya Kirchikov and Tosh Kirchikov. Thanks from the bottom of my heart, Carla. You are the solid rock.

I would also like to offer special thanks to my dear friend and fellow Rotarian, Don Wiginton, who took the time to review my manuscript and made valuable notes and remarks that I incorporated into my book. Your endorsement of my book is a real encouragement for me. Thanks, Don.

I would like to offer my deepest gratitude to our special sponsors: Kay Savage, Glenda Burson, Edward "Eddie" Robbins, and Paul "Buddy" Burson, who brought us to this blessed country as well as other entities and people who helped my family and me on our journey to this country and with our naturalization process.

Finally, thanks to my editor, Liz Reed and her husband, Jim Reed.

God Bless You All and God Bless America!

PREFACE

Year in and year out, food was always scarce and sometimes unavailable in Russia, not speaking about its poor, unhealthy quality when you could find it. I had to go with my family throughout our neighborhood and farm fields in September to October each year and hunt for "green" walnuts from one tree to another and bring those walnuts home in a bucket, peel them, dry, conserve and save them for the winter. Those walnuts were among the most delicious, nutritious, and available food items that we could find and save for the harsh winter season. If you come today to my home office, you will still see walnuts that I bring in every season and save to remind me of my roots, my past and of the very real hardships that my family and I endured in my birth country as well as the blessings of freedom, liberty and plenty that are bestowed upon us in this great country.

"The Russian Dream" was to find a legal way out of the USSR for a better life in a Western country. It was next to impossible for most Russians to perform the legal formalities required to exit the country, primarily because Russia did not sign the Universal Human Rights Declaration until late 1980s, and because of the country's omnipotent, Iron Curtain, Iron Fist-Stalinist regime. My children and I are most proud of the most meaningful accomplishments in our lives and becoming naturalized as the United States citizens.

In Russian and other countries' folklore, fairy tales, and poetry were typically associated with the image of the walnut tree (often confused with the oak tree in Russian) with strength, power and source of energy. For example, in a well-known fairy tale about prominent Russian epic heroes (mighty warriors) Ilya Muromets and Nikita Dobrynich, called "bogatyr" in Russian on their way to a crucial battle, the men stop for a short recess by a mighty walnut tree to rest and heal their wounds. Per the fairy tale, the men were rejuvenated and reenergized after their break under the walnut tree and were ready for the new battle against the sworn enemy; they won that crucial battle. This is one of many stories involving the mighty walnut tree and its nuts that can be found in many countries. The image of the mighty Russian walnut tree or any walnut tree sends a powerful message to the readers. Walnuts by their own nature are sturdy and strong nuts compared with other regular nuts that we eat daily. As we know, the wood from walnut trees makes very good sturdy furniture. Walnuts on my bookshelf are constant reminders of the past, of my roots, my origin, the hardships that we as a family conquered, and the gratitude for the blessings that this great country offered us. Walnuts on my bookshelf are my citadel, my castle, my warriors, my allies as they are here, they are with us for good, forever.

In another tragic and heroic legend referenced in the poem by well-known Bulgarian poet Evtim Evtimov (*"Batashko Klane"-"The Massacre of Batak"*), the main heroes are involved in the national liberation war against five hundred years of the Ottoman Empire's oppression of Bulgaria. In the poem, a soldier's girlfriend had walnuts in her hands and was on her way to take them to the mountains where her boyfriend was an active member of the Bulgarian freedom fighting, guerilla rebel detachment, and was hiding high in the mountains. She was detected and intercepted by the Turkish Ottoman janissaries and was murdered like many thousands of innocent Bulgarians during the infamous Batak mass murder. The young girl fell victim of the nationwide liberation war against the fifth century old Ottoman Imperial oppression, but her struggle and participation were not in vain as they bore the fruits of freedom which actually resulted in the Russo-Turkish war in 1877-1878 that liberated Bulgaria from Ottoman slavery.

As the night drew upon Batak, the girl's relatives and friends found her body. She had demonstrated great willpower, a strong desire to help the countrymen's liberation war against the Ottoman oppression and a staunch dream to see her beloved country free to be the torch bearer of liberty. She was secretly buried as a heroine with walnuts tightly wrapped in her fists. As time passed, many young walnut trees grew up and bore many walnuts that were so much needed for Bulgaria's liberation war. Those walnuts represented the fruits of freedom and provided nuts for the freedom-fighting rebels.

This tragic legend is closely related to the horrendous massacre of Batak, known as "Batashko Klane" in Bulgaria, which was carried out by the Ottoman Empire's troops against the Bulgarian innocent and unarmed local residents. The Ottoman Troops' bloodbath was staged as revenge against innocent Bulgarians for their support of freedom-loving insurgents. My freedom-loving ancestors were so eager and thirsty to experience the fruits of freedom and constantly dreaming about it and could not tolerate the eternity like Ottoman Empire oppression. Two hundred years ago they decided to load a boat with their belongings, sail down the Danube River and settle down as immigrants in Bessarabia, in the same community where I was born.

It is amazing how legend finds its actual way and solution in real life. My story does not end up with my ancestors' drive, indomitable spirit, staunch dream, eternal desire to escape the suppression, and seek freedom and liberties somewhere outside their home country. Their birth country was wronged, insulted, abused, oppressed, and brought to its knees. My ancestors' choice was very clear—life on your knees, life under oppression and slavery were not for them, it was not their choice. Their choice was the one they made and that my family and I are so grateful for-- the choice of freedom. They were not going to compromise as it was not on their agenda.

My father told me and my siblings several times that our grandfather's family on my paternal side planned to come to the United States and settle down as immigrants in late 1920's when Bessarabia was part of the Monarchy of Romania, where they, my parents and grandparents, my siblings and I were born and lived. For some reasons their plan did not come to fruition. I do not know the reasons as it may have been visa arrangements, visa quotas, application procedural issues, qualifications, particular country quotas, the status of Bessarabia, job qualifications, skill sets, and pandemic diseases as there were many reasons families were not able to leave their homeland. My grandparents did not get a chance to come and live in the US, but two generations later my family and I were fortunate to be sponsored to come to this blessed country with our sponsors' help and to pursue our American Dream.

Yes, The American Dream is still alive and well and my family is blessed to call America our home, sweet, hospitable home. Our sponsors were very courageous, persevering, enduring, and unwavering in their determination to get us out from behind the "Iron Curtain." During tough times in the USSR, it seemed that hope and faith were fading away and another dark period of Communist dictatorship was landing upon our family (the failed coup d'état on the Gorbachev Government on August 19, 1991).

I will never forget when I got a phone call from one of our sponsors, Kay Savage, who said: "Peter, I am ready to fly to Kiev,

Ukraine and deliver plane tickets for your family, so you can come to this country and start your employment with University of Alabama in Birmingham…" The entire process coming to this beloved country took fifteen months. For my family, it was a lesson in courage, perseverance, determination, and to never, never, never give up. God opened the doors and led the way, while, our sponsors gave us a ray of hope, a bright light in the kingdom of darkness called the USSR. All the sponsors and their families worked very hard to make it possible to rescue my family from the tyranny of the Soviet totalitarian and dictatorial regime. They made it possible for us to make own American Dream come true and live in this great country as new Americans.

How did you get lucky enough to be sponsored?

FOREWORD

In Walnuts On My Bookshelf, Peter Kirchikov brings a unique and brilliant analysis of communism during the USSR. As a historian and linguist who lived through the empire, he adds to scholarly research his own personal experiences and perspectives that give the reader a sense of the heavy burden communism inflicted on its unfortunate captives. Yet, Peter's personal journey also describes the human struggle to escape from bondage and to live in freedom for himself and his posterity. The book gives valuable insight into the struggles in Russia today to escape another authoritarian regime. The USSR that Peter was born into in 1952 was a brutal, oppressive, totalitarian regime which did not value its citizens beyond exploiting them for the state's benefit (Communist Party Rulers' benefit). The KGB controlled all walks of life and every decision made on behalf of its citizens. Hence, the KGB monitored everyone. Peter always felt he was being watched, as the KGB always knew the exact time of his arrival at his destinations, maintained a list of his personal friends and relatives. The oppression and surveillance in Russian society gave rise to numerous malaises, including rampant alcoholism, drug use, and depression. Between 1940 and 1980, the USSR experienced the highest rate of increase in the amount of alcohol consumed per person among developing countries. Consumption increased by 600 percent while the population grew only 25 percent. By 1980, the average Soviet family was spending 25-50 percent of its monthly food budget on alcohol (Knaus, 1981). Food was always scarce and of poor quality. Families scavenged forest and fields to survive. Peter's family developed the habit of hunting for green walnuts in the countryside around them to secure the calories necessary to survive another brutal Russian winter. They brought them inside to dry and provide nutrition through the long, dark, and cold winters, hence the title of this book, "Walnuts On My Bookshelf."

Every Soviet citizen bore the fear of the Gulag, the hellish prison camp in Siberia. Millions were sent there to suffer and die. This fear of bondage served as a chain to hold citizens "in their place." The KGB attempted to entrap citizens in some petty offence to hold them hostage to imprisonment and require them to spy on their family and neighbors for offences to entrap them as well. Fear of the criminal justice system *how ?*

drove this macabre industry. The KGB knew Peter wanted to immigrate and sought to entrap him in some offense to make him ineligible to emigrate. Peter avoided the "honey-traps" and other plots to destroy his reputation and profession as a guide-interpreter. It required trusting no one and complete discipline in what he said, even in the most unguarded moments. Even in the tragedy of Chernobyl whose aftermath took the life of his young son, criticism of the state was not tolerated.

      Out of this crucible arose an indomitable spirit with a thirst for freedom that had been up swelling for several generations in his family. The oppression and family lore of the quest for freedom was whispered in his ear as he grew up. His sorrow and regret that his grandfather's ambition to immigrate to America had been stymied by an unknown peril steeled in Peter an overriding determination to make it to freedom for himself. Walnuts On My Bookshelf chronicles his personal journey through the labyrinth of the USSR to America. The book also chronicles the healing of a bruised and damaged soul determined to live above the hand he was dealt at birth in the Ukrainian village of Krinichnoye under Communist domination. In writing this book, Peter has exposed the demons of the USSR and has exorcized them from his own soul. The reader of Walnuts On My Bookshelf will be transformed by Peter's ripping the veneer of propaganda off the USSR to reveal this malignant tumor on the 20th Century. This Communist beast marched under the banner of equality and justice, but enslaved its citizens and many other nations. Its advance was stopped by free people joining hands to resist oppression. The Cold War was worth fighting and there was no option but to win it at whatever cost. Peter's book gives us a view of our fate had we failed to win the Cold War. Walnuts On My Bookshelf is a must read for any serious student of the 20th Century!

Don Wiginton, Esquire
Wiginton & Wiginton

My Life Before 1991

My Experience Living in Communist Russia

"I know thy works: behold, I have set before thee an open door, and no man can shut it." Revelation 3:8 KJV

Can you imagine your life without running hot and cold water, without groceries, without a grocery store in your neighborhood or even your city or life without a private car?

Can you imagine your life without Christmas and without Christmas celebrations and all the joy and gifts that come with Christmas?

Can you imagine living in a city of the size of the Birmingham, Alabama Metro area with population about a million citizens with a total of only ten restaurants?

Can you imagine arriving at your office in the morning, and you leaving your coat or jacket on a hanger then leaving your office to go hunting? Not for deer, turkey, fox, partridge, or peacock but for food and items of bare necessity: bread, soap, salt, sugar, shampoo, matches, milk, and dairy products? My parents and I did not have to imagine it at all as we lived a life like that in Communist Russia.

Did you ever wonder when you were a child what the children in the Soviet Union were learning in school or what games they played? Did Russian children all believe that Communism was good and did all the kids believe that there is not a God in heaven as the government wanted them to believe? Did the majority of children accept having to make and drink vodka and wine as a part of life?

I can answer these questions because I grew up in Communist Russia. Though the government tried time and time again to make its people conform to the Communist regime, rural families like mine still practiced Christianity in our home, away from the Omni present Big Brother ears and eyes of the government. Although we were dirt poor by American or Russian standards, I did not realize it as all the families in the village were struggling and poor. That was the way of life in the villages in the Ukraine. We were not free to travel to the beach neither in the summer, nor to the mountains in winter. My parents never flew on an airplane, rode on a train, or owned a car. They did not give me and my siblings Christmas presents on Christmas Day. It was a special treat just to have a nice dinner. One had to work at least six days a week to have food on the table so that when the harsh freezing winter set in the family would not starve. However even with all my parents' efforts to shelter and feed their family, they still lost two of their children to starvation prior to my birth.

Russian children had little time for dreams between all the tasks and chores that were expected of a child including babysitting one's siblings and feeding the animals. Nevertheless, when I dreamed it was about places, people, and things which I had never seen but only read about in books. My books kept me company and fueled my hopes, dreams, and aspirations to leave the only home and country that I had known. I kept these thoughts within me as my parents had never even left the village. I clung to books as evidence there was a better life. My sheer determination, my profession as a translator to tourist groups, and my strong belief in God served me well.

Lenin's Legacy

"I would not like to be a political leader in Russia—they never know when they are being taped."

President Richard Nixon after visiting the USSR

Communist Russia was notorious for the unparalleled, unsurpassed number monuments to the notorious icon of all ages - Lenin. There were more monuments, busts, and statues to Lenin in Russia and other Soviet satellite, subservient countries, than anywhere else in the world. It would have been prudent to spend those funds on food and feed the poor, struggling population of Russia. After seventy four years of Communist regime and seventeen years after the collapse of the Soviet empire in 1991, the fascination with Lenin is still a hot topic, a heated debate in all sectors of population and government: should Lenin's body be kept in the Mausoleum as an icon or bury him in the family plot in St. Petersburg, Russia? Russian propaganda instilled the mantra that was repeated every day to every Russian during the Soviet era: Lenin lived, Lenin is living, and Lenin will be living. But many Russians whose relatives, loved ones, family members were murdered and destroyed by the Communist regime and Stalin dictatorship would seriously argue about this and have multiple charges and claims against the barbaric Communist system.

In Russia – Long, Long Lines

"There has always been a huge confusion and misunderstanding in that mysterious and mystique land of Russia as for eternity, immortality, and immorality."

Peter Kirchikov

Why must Russian citizens wait in the long lines in the USSR? Because we did not have a choice as I repeat this phrase quite often and it is true. If you wanted to feed your family, your children, your parents, yourself, you needed to line up, because waiting in long lines was just part of hunting for food and other basic necessities. Waiting in long lines was a matter of survival, part of life imposed by that system. Everyone had to wait in different kinds of lines to stay alive and to provide something for the family. There were different types of lines we faced in the USSR, not only the food lines, but waiting at the notorious OVIR, Soviet Visa Exit Permits and Registration Office; waiting at the Soviet Aeroflot ticket office to get that dream air fare ticket that finally, and hopefully will take you to the free world and out of the Soviet hell. The mandatory lines were part of Soviet official celebration demonstrations and rallies with long lines where people were fist fighting, wrestling, arm twisting, pushing, shoving, hitting, kicking, kick-boxing, knocking down, bleeding and grabbing inappropriately for any part of your body, spitting into your face for any and no reason. There was no law enforcement when you needed them, no police station around at such moments.

Waiting in the long, long lines wasted a significant part of our lives in the USSR. Sometimes a sales clerk (called seller) will stop the sales process and call for order or ask customers to observe order and only after order was restored would he or she resumes the business operation. Long lines where children of early ages (five and six years old) were obliged by their parents, like a type of chore, to wait for many hours in those long, long lines, often to come home empty-handed, with nothing. Parents expected their children to bring home some food items, purchased at the battlefield of waiting lines and fist fighting, pushing, tackling and shoulder shoving. It is true. Waiting in long, long lines was part of my Russian childhood.

Every time I went to the store or had to wait in lines in any Soviet city, I always carried in my pocket the "avos'ka." Avos'ka is Russian for a net or mesh shopping bag that everybody used during the Soviet period in the USSR for shopping. Many Russians carried avos'kas with them daily, always in their pockets, purses and shoulder bags. They were like 24-hour soldiers, always ready to pull out the avos'ka and shop. Avos'kas became the staunch and unforgettable symbol of the total failure of the Communist system, including the Soviet empire. Recently I saw a video of the benefit concert of the 60th anniversary of a former Soviet, now Russian, and pop superstar. As a joke and to refresh the collective Soviet memory, one of the participants in that show gave as a gift to that ex-Soviet superstar the notorious avos'ka as a reminder of the daily long, long lines and our past daily struggles to survive.

I have very vivid memories of waiting in long lines in our village stores, small shops of about fifteen feet wide by eighteen feet long, where I lined up with a crowd of twenty to thirty people waiting in line to buy milk, bread, sour cream, sugar, flour, soap, or fish, or meat. As young as five years old child; I could not compete and fist-fight and wrestle like the adults and by the time all the strong adults went through the line, there was nothing left as all the food and goods were sold out. I would go home empty handed. That was not good news for my parents, for my siblings and myself because they all expected food and other basic necessities. That meant I would be in trouble and our family would have a problem. There was some type of mild punishment for me coming home without food items, empty-handed with yelling, haranguing and frustration.

Years went by and even my oldest son, Ilya, waited in lines for milk, bread, sour cream, sugar, flour, and soap while I or his mom waited in another line for something else. We did not have grocery stores in the village in Ukraine where I grew up. The population of that village was between five thousand to seven thousand citizens, depending on the times. There were only two shops which sold very poor quality canned foods, juice, candies, crackers, cookies, and bread. The quality was poor to the extent of unhealthy for consuming and poisonings were usual in that society. The first bakery in our village was built in the mid-1980. It could not provide enough bread for such a huge population. Long, long lines, both in the rural and urban areas, for bread, milk, sugar, meat, sour cream, soap, toiletries, and salt were a normal picture during the entire Communist regime period. It is shocking to the Westerner, because the collective farmers were the ones to produce all the agricultural harvest, goods, grains, and cereals, but they were the hungry, the hungriest, like most of the ordinary Russian citizens were at that time. My Russian one-line witticism: All Russians were equal under Communism--equally poor, equally underpaid, equally mistreated, and equally defeated

You go and stay in one line for bread, in another for butter, in the third for meat and sausages. You pull out a book or a newspaper and start reading in order not to waste your time. You get used to reading "between the lines." Russian used to be a well-educated and well-read nation, in part because of lots of lines and a lot of reading "between the lines." Russians are well-known for being avid, patient readers. "Reading between the lines" taught Russians to use the Aesop language of writing witty, well-crafted, hidden messages. They needed the outlet of humor to survive the Communist regime and the environment of totalitarian control, persecution, censorship watchdogs, media brainwashing, and destruction of the opposition, of religion, of dissenters and refusniks, harassment, imprisonment and mockery trials, horrors and brutalities of the Gulag labor and prison camp system.

Waiting in Line at the Recycle Station

One more unique phenomenon of the Soviet Communist system: recycling glass bottles of different sizes, shapes, weight, volume, capacity. Glass bottles used for sunflower oil, medicine bottles, milk, alcohol, vodka, wine, champagne, liquor, and brandy. Families in the USSR diligently collected, stored, and saved all those bottles then put them in a big mesh or carry-all bag and took them to the so-called recycle station store, Priyom Steklotary in Russian. The recycle stations were attached or affiliated with grocery or wine stores and their hours of operation were unpredictable, like everything in the Communist society. Most often such recycle stations were run by alcoholics and other unreliable people. When I lived in Odessa, one so-called recycle station was located in the basement of the attached store. The steps down to the recycle station were very steep and you had good chance to fall down. First, you killed your hands, arms, legs, thighs, calves, wrists and your joints before you brought your glass bottles to the so-called recycle station. Then you had to drag them into the basement. It was another challenge and it was possible you would break some of your bottles or maybe your leg or hand. It all depended how strong or weak you were. You brought your many bottles, let us say 40-50, and lined up (there were always lines for something in the USSR) and you waited because there were fifteen to twenty-five people ahead of you. If you had a child or teenager available you told him to stay in line for you. There, in that line, very often your child would be cheated by some dishonest adult (a very normal phenomenon in the USSR). When the parents came back to the recycle station they would see their son or daughter being pushed almost to the back of the long, long line and there would be a brawl or argument, bickering, or a fistfight. It all depended on the self-worth or the strength and the power of the parents. Calling names and cussing was a normal part of the Soviet life in that situation. Very often there were alcoholics waiting in line and they typically would be the initiators of such fights as they would be the first to oust or remove kids back to the line, and cheat them.

You may ask: why? Why wait in line for so long and possibly get involved in fights?

Here is the answer. Since the USSR was a socialist society and people in the USSR had to pay high for everything socialized, that is, socialized medicine, education, and transportation, people would receive money for their glass bottles to recycle. It added an important little bit to the family budget since Soviet salaries were very low. Typically a glass bottle refund looked like this: about ten kopecks per a small glass bottle, fifteen kopeck per middle size bottle and maybe twenty to thirty kopecks per big sizes of different glass bottles. You might ask: How about other non-glass bottles? There were only glass bottles. Sad enough, but the Soviet industry did not learn during the seventy three years of the Communist system to manufacture plastic or other non-glass bottles. The Soviet centralized government forgot and did not care about its people.

Russian Caviar and Bare Shelves

The caveat of the Russian Caviar is that some goods were not sold openly and were unavailable to the average or most Russian public, but discretely distributed exclusively to the Communist nomenklatura, privileged class, and the elite hierarchy. Working undercover, actually, working "under the counter," hiding, concealing, stashing away most or all food items, meats, bread, even toiletries was the norm of Soviet life. "Pulling out" food items from storage or a refrigerator to sell to the public after a long period of bare shelves was "to throw out merchandise" in Russian, "vybrosit produkti." The term has nothing to do with the meaning of "to throw out," except due to the low, poor, and hazardous quality of the food items which could be detrimental to your health. It was safer to dump or throw out those foods. "Blat," connections, pull or cronyism were essential and needed and still are popular there in order to get some food items that were scarce. Food served as the means of appeasing the hungry and angry, rebellious Soviet people.

Hanging your raincoat or jacket on the chair in your office and going out to hunt for food items was normal for any and every sector and walk of Soviet life. The food stores in cities and especially in small towns, villages and rural areas, were empty. The shelves were bare and ordinary people had to struggle every day to find something to eat and feed their families. Even if they were lucky to find food, the quality was very poor, to the point of hazardous and detrimental to your health, because there were no supervising bodies of the type like the Food and Drug Administration. Big cities, like Moscow, Leningrad, and Kiev were designed by the Soviet government as the showcases of socialism which is why Soviet farmers and their kolkhozs were robbed by the Soviet system. All the produce, harvest, meats, beef, dairy products raised by the farmers were shipped to big cities to mislead Western public opinion and that of the entire world into thinking that the Soviet communist system worked and the Soviet people were happy, which was not true.

While the huge majority of Soviet people were poor and deprived, Communist party bosses and upper echelons were enjoying Russian caviar and their so-called "special packages" of food items from special food stores and cafeterias, called in Russian, "closed stores," more vivid proof that the notorious Soviet system was the Iron Curtain country and a closed society. Those special food stores for the privileged Communist party elite were hidden from the eyes of ordinary Soviet people. You could not find signs or the names of those stores because they were not visible from the outside; they were hidden inside and behind high iron fences and heavy, beefed-up security of the central, regional or local Communist party committee buildings. Their security system was so tight and tough that some of our courthouses in this country may envy them.

It is understandable that the Communist system was not designed to serve the people. On the contrary, the system was designed to rob them, or as Lenin put it from the very beginning of the Bolshevik revolution, to "expropriate," another word for highway robbery. Ordinary people somehow tried to find a way to survive in that atmosphere of working "under the counter," of hiding, concealing, stashing away foods by store clerks, managers and general managers, most or all food items, meats, bread, even toiletries. The Soviet lexicon was real doublespeak and doubletalk.

On the big Soviet red calendar day, November 7, Bolshevik Revolution Day, May 9, Victory Day the Soviet government would "throw out," i.e. pull out from the shelves or storage and sell to the public some food items that would be non-existent for a long or most of the time, e.g. meat, beef, poultry, even toiletries.

"Option Zero" Doctrine

Option Zero was a plan of the Communist government, an ideology according to which to reach the state of total destitute, poverty, failure, fiasco and bankruptcy of the Communist system. In Russia it was called "To reach the point of the brink of an abyss, or to be on the verge of collapse," i.e. total collapse and failure of the Communist system. Originally the "Option Zero" doctrine was adopted by the Fidel Castro government in Cuba calling on the socialist nation to survive at all costs in case of total collapse. It would be safe to say that the Soviet people lived in the Option Zero land and conditions for most of Soviet history and on the verge or brink of the Option Zero of total failure of the Soviet communist system.

Soviet Linguistic Oppression

What is the Soviet Linguistic, Semantic Dictatorial Oppression? You will not find many references about this unique Soviet phenomenon, although it was a very essential and destructive part of our daily life there. The Soviet Linguistic, Semantic Dictatorial Oppression was the official Big Brother Russian language, Sovietspeak, Soviet newspeak, double thought, doublethink, as defined and well-described by the great George Orwell in his immortal "1984." It was the Soviet lexicon used and implemented by the official CPSU, the Soviet Communist party, its officials, its propaganda punitive apparatus, bodies and agencies, by its eternal slaves, including mass media, TV radio, newspapers, publications, writers, reporters, censors, and the main, fundamental law of the country. The USSR Soviet Constitution is the most fraudulent document of all times. The Soviet Communist party and its Soviet Linguistic, Semantic Dictatorial Oppression were designed to cheat, lie, deceive and defraud the Soviet people in order to keep them in slavery during the communist regime years. Moreover, they managed to defraud not only the Soviet people, but to mislead the entire world. It meant the use of the very refined terms, words, phrases, abbreviations and acronyms to promote Soviet Communist ideology, philosophy, doctrines, ideals, Marxism, Leninism, Stalinism, and the material dialectism. They served different types of lies: black and white, half-truths, slander, libel, and provocations.

The revolutions in Soviet bloc countries in 1956 in Hungary, 1968 (Prague Spring), 1980s, 1989, e.g. in Poland, later in GDR, German Democratic Republic and Czechoslovakia raised the issues of the language, how to deal with the words, the so-called "semantic occupation," i.e., of the Soviet Linguistic, Semantic Dictatorial Oppression, its words, press, media apparatus, journalism, its toxicity and their future without it. The revolutionaries wanted to resolve the issue and get rid of the Soviet Linguistic, Semantic Dictatorial Oppression, to be free of it; they wanted free word, freedom of information, of religion, like the civilized Western, free world. The

22

Soviet Linguistic, Semantic Dictatorial Oppression was destructive and equaled the Soviet military occupation in its militarily brutal suppression of the "Prague 1968 Spring" and the Hungarian Revolution in 1956.

My Parents

Per my sister, my father, Kirchikov Kharlampiy Demyanovich, was born on November 8, 1918. My Mother, Kirchikova (Boykova) Anna Petrovna was born August 25, 1916. My mother and my father were married on November 8, 1940. My two older sisters were born in 1943, Kina, and in 1944, Donka. They both died in 1946, during the starvation period after World War II.

My parents' home was a field camp, a battlefield, a place to test your survival skills. We did not have hot or cold running water, central heating, natural gas, electricity, or telephone service. Finally in 1980's, my parents had a two-party phone (you share your phone line with another family in a different house). Christmas-was outlawed in Russia in 1935 by Stalin and replaced with a New Year celebration as there were not any Christmas gifts, Christmas lights, or beautiful Christmas magical decorations.

During the Soviet era, most of the younger generation dreamed of leaving the village and moving to the city to find a better quality of life. There was a huge difference between urban and rural lifestyles. Wanting to move away did not mean one would accomplish that goal. Wanting to move, relocate or transfer was not enough. In order to move, one needed the magic "propiska" or "dwelling permit" from the local government, city hall office, and the police department and a domestic home passport mandated by the Soviet government. One could not get the necessary paperwork and passport without bribing.

In Memoriam of My Mother, Anna P. Kirchikova

A tragic accident took my mother's life but her legacy of love and respect for human life, her love of God, her moral and family values, her optimism and inspiration, open-mindedness, sense of humor and positive attitude will brighten our lives and warm our hearts forever. This legacy affected the lives of all our family members and will endure for many generations to come. My mother was not formally educated but she was the wisest lady in the world. When her oldest sister-in law died during the birth of her baby boy, my mother and my father started taking care of the newborn baby without any second thoughts. My mother breastfed the baby boy while taking care of her two little girls, Donka and Keena, who were toddlers at that time and later died in 1946 as a result of horrendous post-war starvation in the Ukraine. There was never a question in her mind as what to do in this type of situation. Her loving and caring nature for others was clearly demonstrated throughout her lifetime. When her other sister-in law died and left three children orphans, two girls and a boy, my mother and my father Kharlampyi Demianovich Kirchikov again took care of the orphaned children. They provided for them and arranged their stay in the boarding school.

As grown-ups, the nieces and the nephews were deeply grateful and indebted to my mother and father. My mother was five years old when she was hired by a well-to-do family to work for twelve hours a day, seven days a week. She was a baby-sitter and house worker in order to survive and to put some food on the family table. All her life my mother lived in the village and worked hard in the local farm. She was among the first local residents to help establish the farm in 1946 after the devastation of World War II. Her reputation as a knowledgeable, experienced, and hard-working farmer was second to none in the community. She was decorated with Labor Veteran and Best Performance distinctions by the government and featured in the regional newspaper. All our family was very proud of my mother's accomplishments. One of her dreams was to see her children get college degrees which two out of her three children did accomplish.

I will always remember my mom's Southern, Slavic folk songs, her voice, and her messages in the songs. Her songs gave me strength and inspiration. They were treasured values that carried me through my life. I wish I could have taped her songs. She deserves credit for her songs. Her songs helped me not to compromise, never to give up; they were sunshine on a gloomy day. I miss her songs greatly.

Life separated us and I did not see my mom after leaving Russia in 1991. I called my mother regularly since we came to the US, but I did not see her after I left the USSR on September 22, 1991. Whenever I called her, I would ask if she would sing me a song but because of her old age typically she would not sing. However, one night she surprised me and sang my favorite song of a young man, a bachelor facing the tough choices between the beautiful, smart, rich girl and a poor beauty as marriage candidates. Her voice was almost unchanged after so many years.

Whether it was cold winter or spring, our family always cuddled around mom and listened to her songs. When we had family gatherings or celebrations, we always asked our mom to sing and she did so willingly. I miss her ethnic meals also: borsch, the soup with beet roots, cabbage, sour cream, beef, and spices. Very often, it was our first, second and third meal and one of my favorite meals.

My mother had a strong faith, courage, and tenacity. She was Christian and raised her children as Christians. Although she lived most of her life under Communist regime she and our family celebrated all Christian holidays and traditions behind closed doors. In the 1930's, my mother and everyone in the household helped to build the local church in their village Cheshma - Varuiita, now in the Ukraine. My mother and our family attended the church from that time until 1961 when the Khrushchev government ordered to close our village church and banned all church activities, rites, celebrations, and holidays. Our village church was part of the Russian Orthodox Church and had numerous celebrations and holidays in its church activities observed and popular with local church goers and having the church closed down and banning those numerous church activities was a real offense to the God believers and hurt their feelings, spirits, and showed how brutal Soviet government could be. I remember as a young child being woken up early in the morning by the loud ringing of church bells announcing the church service. It was unforgettable. Even though the government shut down the church, they could not stop our family from following our Christian beliefs at home.

Christmas Eve was my mom's favorite time of the year. The whole family gathered around the festive table with ethnic Bulgarian cuisine items and forecast prediction pie. Mom loved this season. She cooked with great desire and always looked forward to the celebration. My father asked the food blessing, praised God for all blessings, and burned incense. The prediction pie, baked by my mom, had surprises baked inside: coins stood for success in finances; wheat grain and sunflower seeds for a good crop and harvest next year; prunes meant a good season for the fruit trees. To bake an unsweetened Christmas pie was an ancient tradition. People wanted to believe in a better, war-free, and worry-free future with a good harvest and success for the whole family and the community. Anna Petrovna Kirchikov loved this time of the year and she dearly loved her family. Her family loved her dearly too. Her loving, gentle, and kind spirit will remain in the hearts and souls of her family. Anna Petrovna Kirchikova was laid to rest on January 10, 2003. God Bless you, Anna Petrovna Kirchikova. We will cherish the best memories of you. Sleep well and good- bye. Our family takes great comfort in knowing you are in His Kingdom forever and ever.

In Memoriam of My Father, Kharlampyi D. Kirchikov

After the death of a relative during her childbirth. my father, Kirchikov Kharlampyi Demyanovich, helped my mother to immediately caring for the newborn baby without a blink of an eye. Loving and caring were his second nature which he showed during his entire life. He is remembered for teaching his children the farming business, sharing his unique expertise, singing folk songs, sharing stories of the historic past. He spent his leisure time with his family, raising his children in a way that helped them grow up to be knowledgeable, experienced, and productive in their lives.

All his life my father worked hard in the local farm. He was the one to help establish, in 1946, the first farm in the community after the devastation, destruction, and starvation caused by the World War II. The first year after starvation the farm had a good crop and it greatly helped the local farmers and the village's starving population. His reputation as a knowledgeable, experienced, and hard working farmer was second to none in the community. He, like my mother, was decorated with the Labor Veteran and Best Performance distinctions by the Federal Government and was featured in the regional newspaper. He and his family were proud of his accomplishments.

One dream of my father's lifetime was to see his children graduate from college and two out of three of his children did indeed accomplish his dream. He also dreamed that at least one of them would get medical doctor training and be able to treat him and my mother if it ever became necessary. Ironically, he did indeed need significant medical treatment because his health significantly deteriorated after the Chernobyl nuclear explosion and he underwent two cancer surgeries.

My father had a strong faith, courage, and tenacity. He was

26

Christian and raised his children as Christians. Although he lived all his life under the Communist regime, he and his family celebrated all Russian Christian holidays and traditions in their home privately. My father worked alongside my mother, other family members, and people from our village to build in 1930's the Russian Orthodox Church in his native village Cheshma -Varuvita, now in the Ukraine. The Kirchikov family attended the Russian Orthodox church from 1930 to 1961, when the Khrushchev Government destroyed the church, disbanded the church staff, discarded the library, and shut down the church. Even though the Communists had the power to shut down the only church in his village they could not, nor did they, stop Kirchikov Kharlampyi Demyanovich and his family from continuing to follow their Christian beliefs in his home. In his family tradition Christmas Eve was also his favorite time of the year. Kirchikov Kharlampyi Demyanovich loved that season and time of year and he dearly loved his family and his family loved him. His loving, gentle, and kind spirit will remain in the hearts and souls of his family. My father was laid to rest in July 2000. God bless you, Kirchikov Kharlampyi Demyanovich. We will cherish the best memories of you. Sleep well and good bye. Your family takes great comfort to know you are in His Kingdom forever and ever!

The Hands of My Mother and Father

"…If God be for us, who can be against us?" Romans 8:31 KJV

The hands of my mother and my father were very unusual. Their hands were the only tools they had and used to make their living. Their hands were their salvation, their way of life, their major assets as the physical value they had to use and cherish in order to take care of the basic needs of the family and bring the food to the table. My parents' hands, especially my father's hands, were scraped, deeply scratched, dried, very dirty, swollen, and covered with calluses and corns. Their hands trembled and shook because they were tired, injured, red, wet, often bleeding, bent, broken, twisted, thick-skinned, deeply scarred and looked like asphalt or pavement. My parents needed a lot of medications for their hands, but the Soviet government and the collective farm industry did not care about the farmers or their hands.

My parents were farmers, or as the Soviet Communist system called them "collective farmers," all their lives. They did not own any of the equipment farmers have in this blessed country. Farming equipment was not available at all in the USSR. All their lives, they had to use very primitive items: shovels, spades, pitch forks, cleavers, chopping knives, hoes, brooms and many other manual tools. It was called manual labor. Very manual. The Latin translation of "manual" is *related to hands and use of hands*. If you analyze all my parents' responsibilities and duties in the collective farm, their manual labor equates to slave labor. Manual labor was typical for the Soviet Communist system, not only for the collective farmers, but for most or all Soviet industries, walks and sectors of life.

My parents used their hands to dig in the dirt, to plant and sow seeds (potatoes, onions, garlic, carrots, celery, parsley), to work in the collective farm, in the vineyard, in vegetable garden, in the fruit garden, in the front yard, in the back yard, on their own small property around their house and to harvest. They worked hard to make their living by using their hands as their only tools. My parents used their hands during excessive heat in the summer, when it was wet and nasty in the early spring or autumn and when it was cold with subfreezing temperatures and gusty and nasty winds in the southern Russian winter. Actually, my parents never had a day off. Officially they were off on weekends, though sometimes they had to work on Saturdays, but all their lives my parents had to work at home, both after work during the week and on the weekends, in order to be self-sufficient and to run their household operation safely. The government did not provide for the farmers; on the contrary, the Soviet government imposed heavy quotas on grain, wheat, milk, animals, eggs, cotton, and rice. My parents had to work every day to self-sustain, including on weekends: to raise animals; pigs, sheep, poultry, chickens, ducks, geese because they could not go, like here in this country, to a store and buy any groceries that they needed or wanted. Grocery stores and drug stores did not exist in our village.

They did not have running cold and hot water, central heating, natural gas or even a bathroom. They used their own wood and charcoal stove and oven both to cook the meals and, in winter and spring, to heat the house. The had to dig a water well, they had to go to the village bath without shower rooms or shower cabins, just to use the common room with tubs taking "birdbaths" sponging off without actually getting into a tub or shower. They had to survive. They were survivalists. The Soviet industry and the government did not care about Soviet people, about my parents, about the average Soviet citizen. My parents, like other people, were not able to purchase or find anywhere in the stores good quality, warm, winter gloves or mittens to protect their hands during nasty subfreezing cold winters in Russia. The best the Soviet industry could offer to farmers were cloth garden gloves that were torn apart in a week or two.

My parents did not wear wedding bands, although for me their marriage was the example of a perfect or nearly perfect matrimonial union. They were loyal and faithful to each other and never contemplated anything contrary to that. I do not remember asking my parents about their wedding bands though I may have asked my sister. Most likely there were no fancy wedding traditions at the time my parents were married in Bessarabia, which was controlled by the Monarchy of Rumania at that time.

Although my parents' hands were always scarred, scratched, and callous, they always took care of their family's basic needs, fed their children, and raised us as honest, hard-working citizens. I am very proud of my parents and their hands. To the best of my memory, it was not a tradition to hold hands and pray, but my parents were devout Russian Orthodox Christians and we used our hands to make the sign of the cross when praying. I am most proud of my parents who raised me and my siblings and gave me the most treasured family, Christian and moral values to help me survive in life and pass them on to my children.

My Parents' Laundry

My parents did not have a washing machine or clothes dryer. How did they wash their laundry? My mother would pack all our family dirty laundry in mesh bags, take one or two middle size metal tubs and my father would drive us all in a horse-driven cart to the Yalpukh lake, about two kilometers from our house. We would unload the dirty laundry, soak it either in the tubs, or right in the lake, on the edge of the water, away from the beach. There was a community beach for the local residents of the village of Krinichnoeyh, Bolgradsky district, Odessa province, Ukraine, the USSR, where I was born. Some people not only from that village, but the adjacent villages, towns, Bolgrad and Izmail, traveled to the beach to relax, swim, and get together, sometimes for school reunion, birthday celebrations, or to fish, then cook that fish. Russians like a fish soup called "ooha."

Back to the laundry: we soaked the laundry in the water and used a so-called industrial commercial soap. I do not believe I have seen anything like that in this country, but I may be wrong. Industrial or commercial soap, in Russian, "hozyaistvennoye mylo," or "household soap" was widely used by the Soviet Russian population. Its purpose was to wash clothes, but since the Soviet industry was inefficient and one would not be able on a regular basis to find and buy a bar of personal hygiene soap, many families in the rural villages, including in my parents' community used commercial soap bars as big as a small brick we use for house construction in this country, or a memorial brick for the Hall of Fame or in memory of World War II veterans. The commercial soap had a beige sand color and bad odor of DDT however I will not describe the contents of the soap.

After soaking the laundry for two to three hours we started washing the laundry items: shirts, underwear, socks, dress shirts, and pants. Some of them were really dirty because we used them when doing the mud bricks, renovating the house, laying down the mud bricks. You needed to have strong hands to wash the big loads of dirty laundry. We did not do this procedure of taking the laundry to the lake to wash it very often. On a regular basis we, my mother, my siblings (my father was too busy to do his own laundry) and I washed our laundry at home. We soaked our laundry items in a middle-size tub in hot water with the same industrial commercial soap bars and used a palm-size rock that we brought from the lake to rub-rub heavily and intensely our dirty clothes. We had to change the water several times to make our laundry clean. This laundry care procedure was a typical way of handling it in that community. Unfortunately, my sister still does not own a washing machine, clothes dryer and she does not have running hot or cold water in the house where I grew up.

Our Galoshes and Rubber Knee-High Boots

Galosh, singular, *galoshes*, plural (also spelled *golosh* or *kalosh*, singular, and *kaloshi*, plural) meaning an overshoe reaching above the ankle, made of rubber, black on the outside and with dark pink cloth inside. Galoshes typically are worn in wet, muddy, slushy, gushy, nasty, severe, horrible, heavy snow-storming, Russian weather. Men, including my father, my brother and I wore knee-high boots which were also made of rubber. I am not a medical doctor, but it is my experience, knowledge, impression and understanding from living in Communist Russia that rubber boots are not good for your feet, for your body, or for your health in general. In other words, rubber boots, including galoshes, are damaging to your feet when worn on a day after day basis. There were exceptions: when females wore knee-high boots they were those female workers at pig farms or cattle-breeding farms as it was practical to wear galoshes in their work conditions. Without galoshes, they would have drowned in the manure and knee-high-deep mud. The men wore knee-high rubber boots with minimal, so called thin-cloth wraps (in Russian: "portiyanki"). Our feet were frozen during the severe Russian winter, during the muddy, dirty spring, fall, and winter. The rubber boots were no protection and caused damage to our health. My parents, like other local residents, suffered certain multiple health problems, including those caused by the rubber boots, galoshes, e.g.: rheumatoid arthritis, called in Russian "poliarthrtitis" – "poli" means "many," also, rheumatism. Both my parents screamed, yelled, and cried for years because of their health problems, including, rheumatoid arthritis and rheumatism affecting the vital parts of the body: back, feet, legs, shoulders, and their hands as they did not have a corner drug store in the village moreover my parents did not any type of medicine including prescriptions or over the counter medications available to them.

Our Parents' House

Our parents' house in the village of Krinichnoye, Bolgradsky Rayon, Odessa Oblast, Ukraine, USSR, was built at the end of the 19th century. We do not have exact records, but over the years it was rebuilt several times. When I lived there, I worked repairing and renovating it. The house still exists. My sister and my nephew currently live there. They have done some major renovations however they still do not have indoor plumbing in my parents' home.

The house was made of mud bricks which were typically used for private house construction, renovation, and repair. The process for making mud bricks and mud brick houses involved only manual labor, no technology. Mud bricks were made, similar to the Mexican adobe, out of mud and dirt that was brought from a landfill or from the area near Lake Yalpukh. The bricks were put in a circle approximately five to seven meters and twenty one feet in diameter. My father managed and supervised most of the mud brick production operations. After the dirt was brought to the home site the next thing we needed was lots of straw to put on top of the dirt. Typically building would take place on Saturday which was an official day off from the kolkhoz however it was a busy, exhausting work day for my parents, all the kids, our relatives and other helpers. My father arranged and paid for a water tank truck from the local kolkhoz to be delivered to the circle of mud, dirt, and straw. A mud circle typically was set up away from the house on the street or behind the street in the open area, a sort of no-man's land, although this land was cared for by citizens of the village but belonged to the kolkhoz (Russian government).

Next, we needed a horse or pair of horses to do the stomping of that mess and mix of the dirt, mud, straw, and water. The truck driver would pump water from the tank through a hose into the mud circle with the straw and my dad, barefoot, with the horse and a whip went many-many times around that mud circle to stomp it down, so it would cure and be ready the next day to make mud bricks. On Sunday, our entire family would gather around the mud circle, plus extended family, relatives and friends would help us. Many villagers were in the same situation, needing to rebuild and renovate their houses. They were very cooperative and would come to help us with the mud bricks work. On different occasions, we would have between fifteen and twenty people working on the mud brick at our house. We returned the favor but no payment was involved, as my mother and other ladies cooked a good fat, delicious lunch consisting either of a chicken and rice or a lamb. We were all dead tired by the time the mud brick work was over,

Then, in the morning the men (I was among them), used the tool called "*motyga,*" a sort of sharp hoe, started cutting that big mud circle into small pieces and carrying those heavy pieces into the molds to make the mud bricks. In a few days after they dried out under sunshine, they became real mud bricks. After the making of mud brick, called "chamoor" in local Bulgarian dialect, we all were exhausted and slept like the wounded. We did not want any more mud bricks. Why? Because in my opinion, mud bricks were not a reliable construction material for building houses with severe weather conditions, gusty winds, rain and heavy snows significantly damaged the structures of the houses. But the process of making chemur was repeated again and again. Mud brick was everywhere in the house except the foundation: in the walls, front, back, left, right, on the ceiling, in the storage room, and in the barn My parents needed mud bricks not only for the house, but also for the auxiliary storage areas, the barn, the sheep house and the stable. Mud bricks were put on the facades of houses.

Houses in the village typically had one room for guests and special occasions and weddings, one small hallway and one living room (for celebrations and parties, Christmas, Easter, wedding receptions), a small hallway, a sleeping room, a winter bedroom, the cellar, a summer sleeping room and zimnik (storage for wheat, corn, peas, beans, barley, sunflower and seeds. We had two barns; one for the pigs (we always had a big pig and a small one), and a hen house. There was another barn was for sheep and lambs. We had a cow and a calf in the 1960's and 1970's. Outside, we had an outhouse that we all dug together with my father, my brother, my sister, and myself. In 1975, my parents invited relatives, neighbors and a local, self-taught expert to dig the windlass well on their property. It was about twenty four meters deep; the average well depth in that area was about ten to twenty meters. Our well water, unlike others, was sour, due to the sulfate in the well and the ground water surrounding the area. You would not drink it but we used it for watering the kitchen vegetable garden, (tomatoes, cucumbers, carrots, parsley) the flowers and the orchard of fruit trees (apricots, apple trees, peaches, plums) and vineyard (different sorts of grapes such as zinfandel) We had poultry with up to twenty to thirty hens with chicks, ducks. (in 1960's) I remember we had also geese earlier. Some of our neighbors had turkeys. The kolkhoz system and the Soviet centralized management socialist system supposed that kolkhoz collective farmers had enough of their own husbandry, vegetable plots, kitchen gardens, poultry, vineyards, and orchards to be self-sufficient and take care of themselves. In reality, the Soviet government did not encourage the above, but tried to destroy such individually owned assets.

The salary paid to collective farmers in the period 1960's to 1980's was a joke. It was very low, even by the Soviet standards around fifty to seventy rubles, approximately eighty United States dollars, per month. The collective farming system could not provide a decent salary, but the kolkhoz did provide allotments of corn, wheat, and sunflower seeds as part of their payment. These allotments were used to feed poultry and domestic animals (pigs, sheep, lamb, and cows). Farmers had enough to feed the animals and could even go to the farmer's market and sell excess supplies which garnered some money to help the family buy more products. (grain, meat, milk) Sheep were cared for by shepherds and herdsmen who were chosen by local area residents.

Surprisingly, such contracts and part-time work arrangements during the grazing season were not supervised or prevented by the governments, both local and regional. Why? Because the agreements were not reported by the parties involved. To my knowledge, per season there would be two to five herds in the village employing totally may be ten shepherds. Still, the Soviet government had control over the situation—those shepherds, with the exception of their helpers who were local school students, were members of the collective farm kolkhoz and as such, they had quotas to meet. They were required to have so many trudodens, and to work so many days per year and weekdays except during heavy snow conditions or inclement weather days. Trudoden is Russian for a work day unit or piece work measure for a kolkhoznik, collective farm worker, to accomplish a specific task.

Quotas were imposed on kolkhozniki and collective farm workers and I remember that the collective farm management kept a strict track of every kolkhoznik's numbers of trudoden per year and talked openly about the performance of each kolkhoznik. At our village collective farm, the team leader chastised some of the village collective farmers for not meeting the trudoden work unit requirements. Not meeting the trudoden quotas was serious business with severe consequences including criminal charges and imprisonment. Such a kolkhoznik was charged with parasitism, absenteeism, loitering, alcoholism, poor health, or any number of other reasons for failure to meet quotas. The record keeping of trudoden was not accurate, which was normal for the Russian Communist system, and the kolkhoznik was falsely accused of not meeting trudoden quotas. Not many remedies for false reporting were available because most of the collective farm workers were illiterate and could neither read nor defend themselves. They would call on their children to talk and argue to the management and look at the parents' work performance records. It is not an accurate statement that after Stalin, trudoden measurements were not used to manage collective farmers. They actually were used.

My Childhood

I have very clear, fresh memories of my childhood. It was a very hard one and I had to work and do my chores from a very young age. At the same time I always tried to find time to play ball with my friends. My mother and father had to work every day from early morning until late evening. They did not have anybody to babysit me. My older brother took care of me and later, of my sister. Demyan is three years older than I am. My mom was not very talkative about our birth deliveries. The medical facilities in our village were very limited. In our village we had only an outpatient clinic called the ambulatory. My mother considered childbirth and delivery a very personal matter which is why reason she did not share much information with us about our births.

My mother's silence about our births was no longer a secret later in life when we were told that we were born in the maternity hospital which in Russian we called a "maternity house." There were no ambulances to call for my mother when she was pregnant with her children. My father took a day off and took my mom to the bus stop in the center of our village. They rode the public bus to Bolgrad, our district center, about seventeen kilometers away from village. Typically it would take about thirty minutes for a bus to reach that destination. Local people did not have private cars in our village. Motorcycles were not very popular. The only means of transportation for my mother was the 30 to 35 seat bus. The buses were always overcrowded and ran late. Sometimes the bus would break down and all passengers would have to wait for an hour or more until another bus, already crowded, would come and pick them up. When it was hot outside it was extremely stuffy inside the bus. Soviet buses were notorious for not having any type of air-conditioning.

My daddy had to make another trip to bring my mother and the baby back from the maternity hospital. Family members were not allowed to wait in the waiting room while the mother was delivering her babies. The excuse was the hospital observed hygiene. My mother did not specify whether I was born in the morning hours or daytime. I think I was born in the night time because all my life I have worked late night and long hours.

My memories of childhood are deeply related to the varieties of chores and responsibilities that we as children had to do at home. As of today I recall forty-two chores. No doubt all the chores did not occur simultaneously, but when combined my daily chores looked like a really hard job. Feeding the cattle was just one of our jobs, especially in the winter when the sheep, cows, and pigs were at home, not pastured by a shepherd. I had to go to the big, tall haystack of dried grass, corn, and barley stacked for the winter as a fodder. Sometimes I tripped on ice making my way there. The animals liked the haystack. They found it a nutritious food. I took their food to the manger, added some corn or food leftovers and while the sheep were eating I would clean their barn. It was really messy in the winter and fall because it rained heavily in fall and snowed heavily in winter.

Some of the sheep would oust the ewes or baby lambs. I would supervise the feeding procedure and be a fair judge. I fed the cattle three times a day. In the summertime we had pigs, cows, and lambs at home. Typically sheep were in a herd, but sometimes my father brought a sheep to be slaughtered for this or that celebration or in observance of a religious tradition such as St. George's Day. It was my responsibility to go around the vineyard, the kitchen garden, and the fruit garden to bring green grass to feed the cattle or to go somewhere to hunt for a fodder of hay. Normally my father took care of the fodder and it was available at home. But my brother, my sister, and I always helped him. I remember working in summers and on weekends, and sometimes even skipping classes at school because the season was in full swing and we had to gather as much food for our cattle as possible.

My father, my brother and I, and sometimes my sister, went to the farm field. Sometimes we rode the farm's horse cart that my father rented for such purpose. Or we could join somebody who had been appointed a certain job and was driving such a horse cart to the field. We settled down somewhere in "gorichkata," a strip of ten rows of trees that served as protection to the harvest in all seasons. We left our "kasholka" which was a wicker food basket that was very spacious. We took our packed lunch for the entire day. It included brynza (sheep milk) and home-made cheese. Sometimes brynza reminds me of feta cheese. We had a lot of homemade bread such as white bread that my mother baked.

My sister, my brother, or I helped her heat the oven to bake the bread. The bag lunch always included a lot of homemade wine for Daddy. I had a flask of water. As we grew up my parents did not mind if we had some wine. In the field our main purpose was to gather as much straw, grass, and corn leaves as possible. All of this was stacked, saved, gathered, and then transported home by horse and cart. It all served as cattle food. We added some fodder and some corn and our cattle were happy. This food was stored for the wintertime. Sometimes the horse cart was so tall that I was afraid to sit on top of it. There were cases when carts were overloaded and they turned over but I remember no casualties.

Animals

My parents had a strange combination of animals in order to survive and had to be self-sufficient as they kept pigs (one or two per season) and also sheep (between ten and fifteen, depending on the seasons). In late 1960's they had one cow, but the Khrushchev government cut all fodder, pasture, grazing and cattle food opportunities and incentives for raising domestic animals nationwide and imposed draconian taxes and quotas on collective farmers to submit dairy, milk, eggs and produce to the government.

Since we had lots of mice and rats in the house, in the backyard, in the hay, grass, grain, we needed cats, not simple cats, but barn cats or as they are called mousers, house watchers, mouse watchers and mice catchers. The same was true about dogs, especially in the villages. Dogs and cats were not kept for pets, but for practical purposes. Watch dogs were working dogs: their duty was to watch the house and guard it from burglars, thieves, criminals, malicious animals, e.g. foxes, wolves, which rarely happened. In my opinion, luckily, our village was almost crime free.

Pomegranates

Pomegranates, delicious and juicy with lots of vitamins, were not readily available and widely grown in the country of my origin. Pomegranates were found only in a few regions and geographical areas there, like Georgia, Armenia, and Azerbaijan where climatic conditions close to subtropical were favorable to grow pomegranates. On a regular basis you could not buy pomegranates as they simply were not available. Only if you went to the private farmer's market on certain days could you find pomegranates, which were very expensive since they were not readily available in any Russian grocery, food stores, shops or anywhere else. The Soviet government did not care about healthy food and its nearly three hundred million citizens.

High prices for pomegranates caused hostility which was raised to the degree of hate by the local population and also nationwide in the USSR, irrespective of the ethnic origin, that is still found as a legacy in the former Soviet countries towards farmers from Georgia, Armenia, Azerbaijan who raised and delivered the pomegranates to the farmer's market. Those farmers had to travel long distances from their home regions to deliver the pomegranates and other citrus fruits: oranges, lemons, tangerines to the major cities of Moscow, Leningrad, now St. Petersburg, Kiev, and Odessa to sell them and make money to pay their hotel stay, and train tickets. Those farmers acted like entrepreneurs at a time when entrepreneurial ventures were illegal according to the Soviet system. There were rumors that there were some underground, i.e. illegal millionaires, thanks to the well-arranged pomegranates and citrus business.

Pomegranates were grown in private orchards on ordinary people's property, in valleys and mountains of hot climate areas of Georgia, Armenia and Azerbaijan. My family, like other families, would buy pomegranates only for our kids, babies and toddlers because the pomegranates are rich in vitamins and antioxidants. We could not buy them regularly because they were very expensive and probably three to five rubles per one pomegranates, which was a very sizable amount of your salary. In the 1980's I was paid approximately a hundred and fifty to a hundred seventy rubles per month so shelling out three to five rubles for a single pomegranate was a very expensive endeavor. Pomegranates are well-known for their tart, sweet taste, ruby red arils. There are many ways to serve pomegranates in salads, oatmeal, cereals, yogurt or your own recipe. I remember when we were lucky to have a pomegranate we would use our hands to split a pomegranate into two then pick arils thus letting the juice pour into our mouths. If you have a bowlful of arils, just pick them with your spoon (or fingers depending on your etiquette) and enjoy them like candies. Actually they are more delicious than candies. I still love pomegranates and enjoy them when they are available. When stored in a refrigerated container, arils will stay delicious and fresh for a long time. You should try pomegranates by all means. My mouth waters all the time I talk, write or even think of pomegranates Bon appetite.

Potatoes

Since meat and foods were scarce and not readily available, the Soviet people were looking for other means of feeding their families. Potatoes were very popular in Russia. You could see long lines at the farmers' markets (private products were sold there) for potatoes. Collective farmers planted and grew potatoes on their own plots of land. They were planted early in the spring, March or April, depending on the weather. They waited till summer to harvest. The earliest potatoes could be picked in June or July. My parents (typically my dad) had to take two days off or wait till the weekend and go to the farmers market in a small or big city in order to sell a few bags of potatoes to make some money in order to buy some food for the family and for the domestic animals. That was part of our survival.

August was the high season for all potatoes "Amerikanka" or "American pink potatoes" were considered to be the most nutritious and the best potatoes along with Vinnitskaya, the name of the regional center in Ukraine-Vinnitsa

The collective farmers packed their potatoes in mesh bags. The weight was about sixty to seventy kilos. My father, brother, sister, mother and I had to carry such big bags. I had to lift many heavy bags and buckets when I lived there with my parents.

In addition to potatoes, we typically grew big size onions that sold well the village was famous for growing such onions. The bags of potatoes were stored at home in the storage area or outside where they got wet when it started raining and that is a problem. To get the harvest to market they needed transportation. Usually they had to hire a truck for four or five families and pay the required fee to the local collective farm management. Some farmers selling not potatoes, but apples, walnuts, tomatoes, plums, raisins, onions (they're not available to ordinary people in stores) would take the train or bus and transport their goods in sacks or mesh bags to the market. When I lived in Odessa, Ukraine, a beautiful, wonderful city on the Black Sea coast, we saw many farmers bringing their goods to our busy, local farmer's marketplaces: "Privoz,"

"Novyi Bazaar" and "Starokonny Bazaar." Odessa was a very popular, busy and bustling seaside health resort, much frequented and visited by Soviet and Western visitors. Farmers, private persons from all over the country from Odessa Region villages, from Ukraine, Byelorussia, the Black Sea Soviet Republics of Georgia, Armenia, Azerbaijan, Abkhazia, Daghestan, Uzbekistan, or Tajikistan. Even farmers from Far East visited our market places. People from Georgia, Armenia and Azerbaijan brought and sold lemons, oranges, prunes and raisins. Those were the only places where tropical fruits grew. The prices were monstrous and biting. No wonder, most of the fruit sellers were supposedly not collective farmers. They made enough money to own their own cars or to stay in the hotels.

The Soviet Communist System did not leave much choice if one did not join the collective farm then one would be in trouble. It was mandatory to be in the collective farm. I lived in the village for almost eighteen years, but I don't remember a single villager not being a member of the collective farm. The management in these Republics had to be more liberal and comply with certain specifics protests, hostility against the Soviet regime. In other words, rules and regulations were loose and allowed them certain concessions as in some of the Soviet villages and town tanks were used several times to suppress manifestations, rallies and protests. You may remember the bloodbath in Tbilisi in 1989, under Gorbachev as I visited Tbilisi on a business trip with a tour group shortly after that shooting.

Praise That Big Fat, Fat Lard

Certain items of our meals in Russia at my parents' home were not healthy food choices. On the contrary the menu could be very greasy like with the very fat pork lard. My parents like other farmers had to be self-sufficient and take care of own their problems including their food since the Soviet government did not care of them. The government took away lots of food staples items from farmers and imposed quotas on meat, eggs, milk, and dairy products. My parents would slaughter a pig in winter and cut the pork into many slices and save them in the cold storage room in our basement cellar which would serve as natural refrigerator since they did not have a real refrigerator until the late 1970's. The pork meat, lard, fat and skin would last a long time, maybe

40

till March and even April, depending on the number of family members at home at the time. It was normal to cut a slice or fat bar three by four inches and take it with bread, plus a few pig skin slices and a fried piece of meat to work or school and it was considered to be a good, healthy lunch. In reality, the food items bumped up your fat and cholesterol levels sky high.

Bill Cosby wrote about his family in his book *Cosbyology Praise the Lard*: "My mother and my father ate oink and they loved oink. And they loved oink grease. Lard is what they ate. And they soaked up grease with a biscuit. So now, my cholesterol is 741! ..." This Cosby piece illustrates well what my family and I experienced in Russia.

Collective Farms

In 1929, the 16th VKP(b), Soviet Communist Party Congress passed a resolution that called for the general purge of the same party. Stalin officially signaled the beginning of collectivization and declared that the party had moved toward the policy of "liquidating the kulaks, well-to-do farmers" as a class.

In the early 1930's, dictator Stalin deported more than a million Soviet farmers across the country as part of his collectivization of Soviet agriculture, a proof of the forced collectivization, since it was carried out against the will of most of the private farmers and as an integral part the Stalin "Revolution From Above" doctrine. More proof of forced collectivization was the deportation of millions of well to do Russian farmers, called "kulaks" in Russian, who did not want Stalin's terror of nationalization of the agriculture and the industry. This movement was known as the dispossession of the kulaks, or also as dekulakization. Nationalization or collectivization of Soviet agriculture and the food industry was forced, or we may call it illegal. I knew families of kulaks in our village who were deported to Siberia and forced to live there in severe, subfreezing conditions. They had problems with Dictator Stalin and Stalin managed to stir hostility toward such well-to-do-farmers. One such family of kulaks lived a few houses up from my parents on the same street. They settled down on our street after returning from the internment, i.e. the deportation to Siberia. Their lives were scarred and damaged by the status of "hated" and "dispossessed" that was imposed on them by Stalin.

Dekulakization means 'liquidation, elimination of the kulaks per the Soviet Dictator Stalin's policy of "dekulakization" of the former Soviet private owners and farmers, called "Kulaks."

After the greatest dictator of all times, Stalin, deported most of the "kulaks," Stalin-made starvation seized the huge USSR called Stalin land, or otherwise known as Staliniada. Kulak, from the Russian "kulak" or "fist." The slang in the pre-Bolshevik revolution era meant "miserly persons who enriched themselves by making others suffer." Bolsheviks Communists interpreted kulaks as peasants who hired laborers to do their work. Later the term was used to mean well-to-do farmer, but in reality at that time the word "kulak" applied not only to those well-off, but also to any successful farmer. Although all those categories of the Russian Soviet farmers: well-to-do, not well-off, well-off, successful farmers, or in between the above categories became innocent victims of the Stalin directive and orders to destroy kulaks known in Russian as "raskulachivanie," "dekulakization," in Russian, i.e., dispossession, elimination of the well-to-do Russian farmers. Between five and ten million people died due to Stalin's destruction of the kulaks that resulted in Stalin-made, i.e., man-made famine due to the disruption of Soviet agriculture, especially in the Ukraine.

More than ten million Soviet "kulaks were deprived, stripped of their land and any and all ownership. Their private property was plundered. Three million kulaks died in the USSR due to the Stalin's directives of dekulakization. After Stalin died, family members of the kulaks who survived the Stalin deportations and deprivations, were allowed under Khrushchev to return to their original home places after huge losses of human lives, resources, funds, property and their own homes and the biggest starvation imposed by Stalin.

"The Revolution from Above" was Stalin's and the Bolsheviks' slogan. "The revolution comes from the masses, popular masses, rank and file, ordinary people, not from the orders of the Communist party organizations." Stalin's malicious doctrine resulted in forced collectivization, forced industrialization, mass deportation and the execution of millions of well-to-do farmers known in Russian as kulaks who were deported to Siberia. Many died because of the severe subfreezing conditions.

Trudovaya knizhka, labor book, i.e. work record, employment record carried by every collective farmer and all entries were made by the collective farm management. My parents had only one entry as they never left the village where they were born and lived all their lives. They worked for the collective farm when it was founded in 1948 after World War II until their last days on earth.

In February 1958, the Khrushchev government abolished the MTS, Motor Tractor Stations, whose tractors and equipment park were used to serve the kolkhozs and sovkhozs (state farms). All the MTS equipment was sold to the kolkhozes. The key word of that period was "restriction" that Khrushchev used to impose on the kolkhoz to restrict the amount of the private land available to the kolkhoz and the amount of food they could sell in the market. This action forced collective farmers to rely more on the collective income and less on the earning from their private plots. That agricultural policy and reform was neither successful nor appreciated both by the farmers and the urban residents who were compelled to shop at the farmer's market since the government stores were bare and empty and the Soviet government was not able to provide or manage the supply of food and staples and basic necessities to the Soviet people.

A Collective Farm, or Kolkhoz in Russian was an agricultural artel. The term "artel" dates back to the 19th Century when it was popular in Russia for associations of independent laborers to get united for collective work with division, working together and sharing the profit and the liability. The origin is Russian. "Артель" came into use in 1884. "Artel" via Italian, "*artieri*" plural, "artisans," "*artier*"-artisan, via Latin –"*ars*"—art. Artel is a cooperative of workers or peasants, farmers or industrial, agricultural workers in the Soviet Union under the supervision of the Soviet government. Collective farms were types of artels started in 1929, after the Soviet Communist Party's 16th Congress that signaled the forced nationalization of agriculture, spearheaded, supervised and sponsored by Dictator Stalin. In this context it is the agricultural producers' cooperative enterprise. Initially there were industrial cooperatives among itinerant workers, but later the practice was extended to collective farms and artisan artels.

A Collective Farm is a huge cooperative made up of fifty percent of the USSR's kolkhozs. To my knowledge, all Soviet collective farms were located in the countryside, rural areas, like ours in the village of Krinichnoeyh, Bolgradsky Rayon, Odessa Oblast, Ukraine, USSR. Theoretically, they were managed and operated locally and internally by the village-based collective farm administration called collective farm management, "pravlenie kolkhoza," but in reality they were heavily managed and governed by CPSU Party entities and organizations. The difference was that sovkhoz workers were on the government's payroll, but also located in the rural, countryside areas.

Pasturing the Cattle

During summer vacations, in the fall and on weekends, it was my permanent responsibility to take care of our cattle, sheep, and the lambs. Usually I talked to my friends who lived on the same street and made plans for after school fun along with my chores. We took the soccer ball and our cattle to the neighborhood free space. The area was not developed and cultivated but owned by the kolkhoz. We used that space for a long time as a soccer field with goals we made ourselves. We played soccer until dark. Some of our parents would come to the field and reprimand us. When we played so adamantly that we forgot about our goal which was to watch our livestock. The sheep would run across the road and graze in the kolkhoz-owned corn, wheat, pea or rye field. The obiezdnik (horse-rider security person) would come on his routine rounds and find our sheep. He would beat us, or take our fathers' names and penalized them. The parents were supposed to pay between ten and thirty rubles for the damage our sheep had done. We would draw lessons from such cases at least until the next time our sheep ran again into the kolkhoz field. I took also books and newspapers to the pasturing sessions so I would take time to read. I loved reading from early childhood.

It was a big hit among us to make our own whips and imitate the full-time shepherds and herdsmen. Our whips were made of pigskin, horsetail hair, sticks and metal rings. When we played, we wrestled and we had our unofficial soccer tournaments between teams from different streets. Unfortunately we did not have referees. Sometimes we played sheep wrestling and teased the sheep pulling them by their horns. Our sheep usually wore one sheep bell. We used those sheep bells during Christmas celebrations for caroling, and sometimes in a sort of show with singing, dancing and pantomiming.

Another favorite game we played was called "shtandur" (freeze). I do not know the exact origin and etiology of this word. I think it's jargon, a lingo term. The team starts a person who throws a ball high into the air and all the team players run away as far as possible. The whole idea is to run away as far as possible because when the thrower catches the ball, he commands "Shtandur," or "Freeze." Nobody moves. It's good if you had the chance to hide behind a tree, electric pole or behind somebody else because after yelling "Shtandur," the thrower is going to aim at one of the players. If that player gets hit and he or she doesn't catch the ball, then he or she will be the next thrower. If the player catches the ball, the same thrower will have to repeat throwing. Most of the guys and girls ran away pretty far so they could not to be reached. We played it any time of the day and evening, late evening, even when it was drizzling and after rain. It was a team game. We had fun, we enjoyed the game. The rules were simple, as you see. I have not seen kids in other communities or towns or countries play this game. We enjoyed running and having fun. It was a sort of hide and seek game.

"Sabachka" or Puppy" was another team game. We had a ball of a size like volleyball, but it was a rubber ball. One of the team players was a loose dog-puppy, hunting for the ball. The other players, meanwhile, passed on the ball to each other. The idea of the game was not to let the "puppy" intercept the ball. If the puppy did succeed, then he took the place of one of the players and he became one of the kids passing on the ball quickly.

We didn't play much because we had so many responsibilities and chores to do on the farm. Feeding the poultry was one of my responsibilities. We had about twenty to thirty chicks, chickens and roosters. There were times when we had ducks and drakes. In the 1960's we had a few geese. Sometimes those geese took pride in flying. Once they flew away from our lawn to the only river in the village. As far as I remember we fed our poultry once in the morning and once in the evening. Typically my mother prepared the chickens' food which was a mixture of corn, wheat, fodder and leftover bread and crumbs. We had a "korito," a kind of feeding container for the poultry. The korito reminded me of life in general; the stronger chickens and roosters ousted the weaker ones, fought with them and took their food. Some of them would stay hungry if I did not watch them and make sure they got some of the food.

Tending the Sheep

Shepherds, one or two of them from our street, had their huts in the fields and were stationed there throughout pasture season (May through September). In October and November our sheep were tended by two people from the same street that skipped their work in the collective farms to take sheep and lambs for the whole day, Monday through Friday. They pastured the sheep in the out-of-village area between fields of corn, wheat and fruit gardens. Strips of woods served as protection for field crops from hail, heavy rain and heavy snowfall. Shepherds were on a contracted salary which was considered to be a very good pay. They stayed in the hut or in a big sheep barn for at least four to five months, away from their families, not being able to take care of their children, family needs, house chores or intimate life. Some of the shepherds had alcohol problems.

A family would come to the sheep house on assigned schedule to milk the sheep and salt the milk to make sheep cheese (similar to feta) which was a very big treat. The family was also supposed to bring food, bread, garlic, onions and ethnic Bulgarian soup.

The milking procedure was verbal agreement between shepherds and the local families that is why punctuality and commitment were not always observed and caused problems. The shepherds' work required that they stayed away from their families and spent all their nights through the season tending the sheep. Sometimes women, under any excuse, would bring food to the shepherds in order to obtain the sheep milk and turn it into feta cheese. Every sheep pen had at least two or three dogs to guard them. Some of the dogs were very mean and would not let anyone ride the horse driven cart or drive it by or pass by the sheep pen. Dog biting occurred often and scared many people in that neighborhood.

The sheep pen and the sheep were in our village in an abandoned and neglected plot of land, not cultivated and reclaimed and not suitable for farming by the local kolkhoz at that time. We pastured our sheep there in between seasons or when we were asked to do so by our parents. During summer vacations our main responsibility, assigned by our parents, was to take our cow (when we had it in the 60's)and the sheep to pasture them out of the village, in strips of woods. We also would take our soccer ball, tennis like balls, and playing cards.

We would forget about the cattle and the sheep. The sheep were happy to run into the kolkhoz owned green corn fields, wheat, pea and sunflower fields, ripe ready to be consumed cattle and kolkhoz fields. Pasturing privately owned cows, sheep and goats was against kolkhoz rules. We were told about it and instructed by our parents. The local ftobiezdnik" called in other Russian communities to catch our cattle. The ezdobon-kolkhoz property guard-horse rider (sentry) asked for our names and our parents' names. We were reported to the kolkhoz management and the chairman of the kolkhoz. Our parents were penalized twenty to fifty rubles, depending on the amount of damage and the mood of the ezdovoy (guard) and the chairman of the kolkhoz. Sometimes the chairman himself made rounds and if he caught us, we would be punished and spanked. My right ear was twisted by our kolkhoz chairman which was very painful.

We traditionally played soccer in an area of our kolkhoz called "granddaddy Peter's well" by the Big Oak Tree we traditionally played soccer. Another game involved throwing a tennis size ball from one player to another while keeping it away from the "dog," a third player whose intent was to intercept the ball.

Cherepinki playing, with tail and coat end, was a primitive sort of gambling we played with our pocket change. It was officially illegal and outlawed by school but big crowds came to see adults play the game on Sundays. Some of players would make money while playing the game. Typically, such games would have two players in the center of the village there would be a big crowd of on-lookers crowding around the players. It looked like a spectacle which is why a policeman would come from the Bolgrad district precinct assigned to our village. His duty was not to allow the game to happen and he would disperse the crowd but when the policeman was gone, the game would resume.

The chairman spoke Russian to us, as most of the communication and instruction at our village schools, "Pravda" kolkhoz, Communist Party and school meetings, public addresses were all spoken only in Russian. Ironically, ninety nine percent of the village population was ethnic Bulgarians.. There were few ethnic Jews. Truth to say, Bulgarian was dialectal, the language of communication among all local residents of Krinichnoyew, most Bolgrad District (county) villages and more counties in the Odessa region, but Bulgarian was outlawed as the language of instruction. Therefore all the TV and radio stations only broadcast in the Russian language..

Family Chores and Responsibilities

Stacking hay, straw and grass as an animal food was a real concern for local residents. Most of them had cattle and had to provide enough food for the animals throughout the year. Since the collective farm and the state could not sustain private household farms with enough fodder and animal food, private cattle owners had to find the way to fund it. Some collective farmers bought animals from each other, however if family members were old then their households were not well run. There were cases when a fire occurred and all the haystacks burned to ashes and the family suffered big losses. The fire station located in the village was not very efficient or very quick because they could not be reached in time of emergencies as there were no phones in our village until the early1980's. Firemen were supposed to detect fires from an observation tower in the village.

Picking fallen fruits under the trees was another of my home responsibilities in summertime and early fall, typically after strong winds or heavy rain. Sometimes hail would cause a mass fruit fall. I had big bucket to pick up fallen apples, plums, peaches, pears, grapes and apricots. The fruits were wet, but not well-washed. I ate lots of fruit and still love eating fruit even today, especially tropical fruits, since they were scarcely available to us as children. The danger was that they were sprayed with a copper anti-insecticidal spray. My father had a special spraying machine, but still, apples and plums were often rotten. Rotten fruit with insects inside which was another lasting impression of my life as a Russian boy.

After the official harvest season was over, farmers of the collective farm were allowed to pick up apples and peaches. No managers supervised this completion of the season but from time to time some supervisors would come and make rounds.

After I collected those fruits either we ate them, saved them for school, dried them or used them as fermentation ingredients for making rakiya, homemade vodka or samogon. Fruits were very healthy and nutritious. I should mention that when there was a severe food shortage in the USSR, people in the villages ate fruits, onions, garlic, carrots,

48

grapes and vegetables, made their own salads and dishes, packed lunches and resolved every food problem.

Bringing Water from the Windlass Well

I remember doing this chore from very early childhood. My mother, father or my older brother took out the water from the street well. It was about seven meters deep. It was a communal well, located three houses up the street from our own house. It was dug in the early 1960's, as far as I remember. After my brother drew the water from the windlass well, he poured it into my bucket, a ten to twenty liter bucket. As I grew older I always carried two buckets of water, one in each hand.

Many boys, including myself, in early childhood age drew water from that windlass well which was not a safe job by any means. One could fall into the deep well and drown. There was not any supervision by the parents as they were gone to work in the farm fields. There were not any baby sitters or nannies to look after the children. We used also to play around the windlass well. We would open the top of it, the cap, and look at the birds' nests as the larks made their homes there.

Bulgarian Traditions

Bulgarian women had four types of headwear: a handkerchief, headdress or a headscarf. All her life my mother wore headwear that looked Greek or Muslim, wrapped all the way around the neck and head, not to be confused with the burka. The ladies my mother's age and generation wore several types of headwear all their lives. Headwear was worn by the females in the Bulgarian villages, communities in Ukraine, Moldavia, former USSR, and several Balkan peninsula countries: Bulgaria, Greece, former Yugoslavia, Cyprus, and Rumania.

There were different types of headwear for the ladies. 1. Casual headwear, typically dark, black, thin, worn mainly in the summertime, in spring and in the fall. 2. Thick, casual, dark, shawl-type, big like a scarf to keep you warm, multicolor black and brown, plus white spots, for winter wear. 3. A headwear for special occasions: weddings, funerals, Christmas, New Year's Day, holidays, saints days like Saints Paul, Peter, Daniel, Dimitrius Day celebrations. I think it was hot and perspiring for ladies to wear such headwear, but they did not complain about it. The history of this headwear dates back five hundred years to the Turkish Ottoman Empire yoke, suppression, and oppression that caused a lot of brutality, immigration, and defection. The above oppression resulted in a widespread national liberation movement and struggle, a guerilla war and subversive actions against Turkish oppressors. It also caused mass exodus from Bulgaria down the Danube River and one of the main channels of the emigration to find shelter and refuge Russia and other countries to settle down.

Holidays

For almost seventy years the Soviet Union was a country of atheists. The Bolshevik Revolution of 1917 began the persecution of believers. The church was under tight control. Many people were forced to emigrate and the Bolsheviks expropriated their lands, estates, finances and businesses. Church assets were confiscated and many clergymen seized, imprisoned and crucified in the churches. Famous churches, monasteries and nunneries were made museums or abandoned entirely. Communism was in control of all spheres of the totalitarian society. According to Solzhenitsyn, 67 million Soviet people were murdered under Stalin and 30 million more perished during World War II. The Orthodox Christmas was celebrated in Russia for the first time since 1936. Until that time, the New Year was the official Soviet holiday when everyone gathered around a festive table and a New Year tree. The Communist leader(s) addressed the nation on TV. A fond childhood tradition was the New Year forecast pie, made with enclosures of coins, plums, pears, straw and seeds, each having a special meaning. Grandfather Frost is the equivalent of the Untied States Santa Claus. Carnivals, masquerades, parties and banquets are held at schools and small gifts are distributed to students (with parents paying costs). Dance competitions and recitals were also held the school. We had some curious traditions, like the washing of all dirty clothes on New Year's Eve, signify cleanliness all year and still abound. There was another holiday tradition which was to dream of good and sacred things on New Year's Eve.

A good treat was to take your girlfriend or wife to dine at a restaurant. It was expensive occasion and seats were easily not available. Restaurants were not numerous in Russia in the 1970's and 1980's as they were here in the United States. Odessa with a population exceeding one million citizens, had only twelve restaurants and most business and government cafeterias were closed for unorganized groups. One could not just walk in from the street and have lunch or dinner at a restaurant as they were primarily reserved only for the tourist groups visiting the city.

During the 1970's it was a Christian tradition to bring food to the church to consecrate or sanctify it, to have it blessed by the priest. I remember a long line of the Russians of all ages with children and babies waiting for the priest to come and to sanctify their food. The food items included stewed meat, meatloaf, beef, homemade bread, rice, cookies and candies. Many people laid out their food items on the sidewalk outside the church, because the church was either under restoration or overcrowded. They spread out a towel or newspaper to lay out the food. Then the priest would come out and consecrate it.

Love and Marriage Traditions and Celebrations

When I think of love and marriage in Russia, I think of the Eighth of March, Women's International Day, as the best display of love and appreciation. It is comparable to the American Valentine's Day celebration of love and marriage traditions. Ethnic Bulgarian weddings as I remember were very colorful and unforgettable. There were fifty to sixty people sometimes up to one hundred, depending on how many were invited and how many came without being invited. The big question about the marriage: is it a matter of love or convenience? My mother was born in 1915, my father in 1918. Their marriage, in the fall of 1937, was arranged by their parents, I believe. My generation, born in early 1950's and later, typically married because of love, although some newlyweds were married off by their parents to a boss's child or a wealthy family's child, even in this day and age.

In Old Russia, the groom's parents typically took kaleska, a treat of cooked chicken, beef or some other meat to the would-be bride's house along with a bottle of homemade wine and discuss details of the engagement. They also took gifts for the bride and the bride's family, for the groom, the in-laws, the best girls (bridesmaids), best man and groomsmen, as well as gifts for other relatives. The same tradition is still observed today. The man tells his parents that the couple's love is strong and it is time to make arrangements for the marriage and wedding reception.

After the family discussion when the groom assures his parents that he is deeply in love with the girl, they go to the would-be bride to ask for her hand in marriage. Sometimes it may be just the guy's imagination that the couple were in love. The delegation heads for the engagement party negotiation only to be turned down if in her own belief, there was not a deep love or enough to result in marriage. In other cases, when both parties were deeply in love then they agree to marry.

The delegation from the groom's closest relatives arrives at the bride's house for the announcement of the engagement, however all expenses belong to the groom's parents. At the future bride's house the delegation meets her mother and father, her grandparents and godparents, and they all discuss the marriage details: the date, the gifts, menu for the meals and the wedding ceremony itself. The bridesmaids and groomsmen are included. Typically, members of the wedding party are referred to as "witnesses" in Russia because they go with the bride and the groom to the marriage office, where they sign the marriage contract.

If the parents of either the bride or groom were in their forties or younger then generally they pay all the expenses to cover the engagement party, the wedding reception, food, and inexpensive gifts. It is not like in America where the bride's family bears most of the burden for the expense of a wedding. If the groom's family was better situated financially, his family paid more of the costs. If the bride's family was financially better off, then they paid the wedding expenses. If the bride and groom's parents were older (in their 50's or 60's) and dependent solely on the government pension, the wedding would be smaller and simpler. If it was a big wedding, the groom's father would bring a sheep, a lamb, or a big pig to slaughter for the special occasion. They would have a meal and drinks (wine and rakiya, a kind of home-made Russian vodka). It would much time, money and effort to hold a wedding ceremony and all the accompanying events. There would be plenty of alcohol and many of the family and guests got very drunk. Everybody seemed to be happy during the four day wedding celebration except the cooks and the bride.

The bride would have realized that love is sweet and good but that love is blind. After the wedding is over, the groom, now her legal husband, and her parents-in-law expect hard, diligent work from the new bride. She is an addition to the family, one more horse in the cart that makes for a stronger family. If down the marriage road the bride does not work hard from early morning till late night and take good care of everything, she could be battered and abused by her husband. Although he may be having a good time drinking wine, samogon (homemade vodka) or beer with his buddies, the new bride's in-laws and her husband may mock her and spread rumors about her if they do not care very much about honoring her as a wife and a daughter-in-law. For this reason, pregnant Russian women were happy if their newborn child was a boy and not a girl as a future wife if could be like slavery.

The tradition of sending wedding invitations started being introduced in the late nineteen seventies but prior to that time was not very popular. When I got married in the mid-seventies we did not have pre-wedding and rehearsal parties nor a post-wedding party, only a party for our immediate families and friends. Church weddings were not practiced in Russia.

The Eighth of March is the only day when Russian women forget about their daily burning problems, concerns, troubles, waiting daily in long lines and hunting for bread, butter, milk,. sugar. soap, shampoo, and many other items that we have in the States in abundance. It is comparable to the American Valentine's Day celebration. Flowers, lots of flowers. I still love giving flowers on Thanksgiving Day, Christmas, New Year's, Easter and especially on birthdays. Russians believe flowers symbolize love, appreciation, and even more adoration. Another way to show appreciation was to write a letter to a radio station and request a song for your woman. There was only one local radio station in Odessa and it broadcast only three hours daily in Ukrainian, Russian, Romanian, and later in Bulgarian. In the late 1980s we did not have talk shows so could not call directly to order a song.

As I mentioned this holiday was widely celebrated and it was also highly politicized. Different official meetings like at corporate and local levels were held and gifts or awards were presented to the best women employees. Internationally acclaimed female public figures were invited to visit the USSR and participate in the celebrations--e.g., Indira Gandhi of India or Passionario of Italy. There were gala concerts for these occasions with the best performers and entertainers involved. Women's Day in Russia is a once a year celebration and fiesta is underway at full swing. Long Live Love!

The gifts could have ranged from perfume (Soviet made and if lucky then one could find Western-made), dresses, lingerie, a box of chocolate candies, a replica of a painting (if you could afford one) or hand-made crafts and arts items such as woodcarvings. Gifts differed and depended on the age and relationship between the people. They were relatives or family members, wife and husband, or boyfriend and girlfriend, or stranger-in-the-night-train-car- compartment, or partying in the hotel restaurant at the corporate business meeting. And books. Russians love books very much! A book gift could accompany or be a supplement to any kind of gift.

On the Eighth of March you can see many well-dressed ladies, well-groomed, pretty women, mothers, grandmothers, daughters, granddaughters and great-grandmothers along with a sea of flowers, smiles, gifts, cakes (one of the best treats for the occasion) at parties at restaurants, cafes, lunchrooms and cafeterias, toasting (Russians love toasting). It is their big, big holiday! Once a year holiday! There was a river, a flood of alcohol on that day.

Alcohol has been the major article of income in the USSR since Stalin assumed the power. Alcohol made more than seventy million Russians permanent alcoholics, though that was not reported by Soviet official statistics. We did not have AA (Alcoholics Anonymous) in Russia. Alcoholism in Russia is considered a crime, not a disease. This is why it is not treated. When we arrived in the United States in September, 1991, one of our sponsors took us to grocery in our neighborhood. I thought the grocery was the only one in the Birmingham Metro area and that most of the fruits, including tropical fruits, were available only during the fall season. Since then, every day brings me surprises of discovery and reminds me that the Soviet media coverage of the US reality was very biased.

Life, love and accord, adoration, devotion, loyalty, peace and mutual understanding, respect, honor, reverence, consolidated efforts were the best and most appreciated values that Russian families tried to incorporate and implant in their children and grandchildren. While I lived in the USSR, from 1952 until September, 1991, courses for newlyweds and would be families were offered by radio, TV, marriage

54

offices (in Russia, the Palace of Nuptials) and doctors' offices. The courses were meant to strengthen families and boost the above-mentioned values. When I think of love and marriage, I think of the Eighth of March, Women's International Day, as the best display of love and appreciation. That holiday has been widely celebrated and is still popular with Russians. Preparation for the celebration takes a long time because food is scarce and buying gifts is a real hunt that lasts for several days. Often the hunt ends with no results.

The hunt for medical was often met with no results as well. We had a relative who had been a nurse and had connections with doctors and pharmacists. She lived in downtown Odessa, knew many people there and had many patients. But still we had problems finding pills, ointment or suspensions for my children. Chiropractors were not recognized in the USSR. Chiropractic was illegal in Odessa although I remember there was Doctor Kasiyan in Poltava who was a chiropractor. He was very popular because he was very successful. There were long lines of patients coming to see him from remote parts of the USSR, from cities, villages and towns. They had to wait day and night, camp around his house, sleep in the park or on the streets or stay in hotels, if there were rooms were available. Dr. Kasiyan tried to help his patients who traveled long distances to see him. Most of them were poor, old, disabled and not covered by the Soviet law. He paid for their hotel accommodations, for their food and travel expenses.

During my childhood one of my second cousins fell from a tall oak tree as a teenager and hurt his back badly. Unfortunately, as of today he is still disabled and in pain; such is the nature of health care in Russia.

Telephone Service and Customer Service

How closed was the Communist society? Very closed. Here we go: we had to call an operator for long distance, calls were dropped, conversations were cut off and bugged, buzzing noises were always eternal attribute between the callers. We could not afford one simple, much needed important helper if you were to make an international call which was the international operator. As late as 1990's, you could not pick up the phone and call the international operator and place a call to United States or another overseas country. In order to make an international call, you had to take street car or a public bus, change to a trolleybus, then walk downtown, in old town of Odessa, go to the busy main post office (central post office or POSTAMT, a very German word). You had to line up there at Postamt as there were always lines, everywhere lines in Communist Russia. I got used to reading between the lines and my wife says, I am also good at reading people (she always wants to make me feel good, she is really sweet). We lined up in a queue to place an order for an international call for example to our American sponsors in the United States. It took approximately thirty to forty five minutes to place the phone call. You paid your fee, got your receipt, and you think you are lucky you got through this? The Postamt clerk told you, that there is another long, long line to make international calls and your turn for your international call was lined up and you would get the appointment to make the call in thirty four days. You drop your lower jaw and everything else that you can and you go home. You have a strong desire to run away from that hell called Postamt and the USSR, but you are lost, you cannot find your home, you use the public phone; no, first you had to line up to use the public phone and call your wife to help find the way home, since there was no GPS, no Google maps or any devices like that. You are at home, finally, sitting, eating, very stressed, actually depressed and wait and wait for thirty four days for your international call appointed time. Finally you hear your phone ringing at the scheduled hour, thirty four days later; you even hear the international operator heavily breathing booze into your ear; you glorify her, you grab the phone and your phone-lover (the international operator) is there, right there, calling you. 'No, no," the international operator says, "your party did not arrive at the notified time and nobody is answering the international call on the other end of the phone line."

Lie, liar-liar as with the KGB's manipulations and operations. That is the true name of the action where an international operator was actually paid for and serves as valuable asset and a KGB operative. The vicious circle resumes, you cannot renew your international phone call order as you are a repeat customer. You go back to the end of the line at the Postamt. That is the rule. The rule of thumb. Thumbs up, Mother Russia.

The Russian Bathhouse-Banya

In rural areas Russian homes did not have bathtubs or showers; rather, bathing was done in a community bathhouse which was owned by the government. A typical community had 5,000 to 7,000 people and only one bathhouse! A staple of the Russian bathhouse was the weeping willow brush. Instead of a tub, the bathhouse had a very hot, steamy bath with a table. A family member or friend would rub your back with a brush made of weeping willow branches, then paddle your back and wrists, after which you would run out of the hot steamy bath to a snow hill and either rub yourself with snow or throw your body into the snow. Our village bathhouse had two shower rooms with one for men and another for women. Children used the same shower rooms with the adults. The bathhouse was open twice a week, on Friday evenings and Saturdays. During the week we heated water on stove in a pot, went to the backyard, took off our clothes and washed our bodies with soap. My American friends freeze when I tell them this story. Typically, groups of friends, family, acquaintances, even strangers gathered at the bathhouse as drinking alcohol was a central part of the bathhouse community.

Alcohol was an important element of bathhouse communities and rituals. One, two or three bottles of vodka or locally made wine or beer appeared on the scene. Alcohol was always used by Russians in different various community activities. It now well known by the medical profession how excessive alcohol drinking can effect a person. The Russian homemade vodka was an extremely strong alcohol drink which would not have ever met the United States' standards and requirements for consumption to any individual.

In the 1930s, Stalin created the alcohol industry as a principal agency of revenue for the country. Unlike the United States government which supervise, test, and insures the quality of production, Russia had no such safeguards. Lack of control meant that there was no standardization. Even though it was against the law to produce alcohol, Russians produced vodka in much the same ways Americans produced "moonshine." Nevertheless, it was common for groups of Russians to drink homebrewed vodka in great quantities. The Russian culture is associated with heavy drinking, in part because of the importance of revenue from alcohol sales, in part because of the oppressive environment, in part due to peer pressure. In addition, there were no sodas, no juices and very little safe drinking water, thus alcohol became the primary beverage, even for children. In business settings, people who did not drink were distrusted as not being part of the morale of the company, as traitors to the culture.

In the midst of this cultural phenomenon, people who developed alcohol-related problems were deemed criminals by the society, by the medical profession, by business and the government. There was no understanding of addiction; there were a few treatment centers in big cities, but the average rural Russian had no access to help with alcohol related issues.

We did not have an organization like the US Federal Food and Drug Administration and the sale of alcohol was always considered by the Soviet Communist Government Party as very essential revenue for the Soviet budget. The Soviet Party did not care about health, morale, moral values, family well-being, earnings, work conditions, general safety or traffic safety of the Soviet people. The attrition rate in business was very high due to problems related to alcohol.

Northern Coast of the Black Sea and Medicinal Mud Baths

I have not come across such a medical treatment in the USA or other countries I have visited where we had medicinal muds. There were health resorts in Kooyalnik, Luzanovka and Lebedyovka, where our college sports, recreation and training facility were located. People came to these health resorts either advised by their doctors or on their free will. They all were looking for cure of their pains and aches such as backaches, spine, hip, shoulder, joint and internal health problems. There was a black colored mud that patients found on the bank of the Black Sea North Coast which they rubbed into their skin throughout the body, from cap-a-pie, from toe to head. They were all black and reminded me of Halloween party costumes. They believed in the magic healing force of the medicinal mud baths, as well as their physicians who prescribed this remedy. The medicinal mud had soothing, sucking, massaging, perspiring qualities. If your feet were stiff or you had arthritis, doctors recommended these medicinal muds. The list of diseases was long and we must keep in mind that the levels and standards of Soviet medical service and healthcare providers were low and pharmaceuticals were not always available.

Public Toilets

It's not a pleasant subject to write about Russian toilets or public bathrooms. They were filthy and extremely stinking. There were no cleaners or chemical remedies to fight the bad odor. There were many times that it was worth it to wear a gas mask when I got into a public bathroom. Public restrooms were rarely found in some areas and neighborhoods in Russian cities. The bathrooms were not safe at all to use. Crimes, rapes, murders and extortions happened very often. Public facilities were not well-lit. Young girls, students, ladies were not safe alone; they were advised to walk in groups of two or three people to avoid or prevent crime. Many alcoholics, drug abusers, chemical abusers used public toilets to do drugs, to meet their buddies, to party, to drink alcohol. Sometimes they had sex typically with prostitutes. Public bathrooms were also used for black marketing, selling or exchanging goods like candies, chewing gum, condoms, clothes, gloves, shoes, socks, food items, canned foods, presents, underwear, briefs, lingerie, sleepwear and bras, even tennis and other sports items.

A funny story was popular when I lived in the USSR: an old rich Frenchman was dying. His family members and would-be survivors assembled around his deathbed.

"What is your last wish before you go to the better world?" they asked.

"Build a public toilet in the downtown area of Paris," he responded.

I do not know if Paris needed an extra public toilet but I am sure the rich Frenchman had enough money to build a public bathroom. I know for sure that Russia needed much money to build enough public toilets to stop seeing troubled men squeezing their hands in their pockets, dancing, prancing in search of a toilet and peeing openly in the bushes, shrubs and by the trees like dogs.

Here in the United States, if you need to use the bathroom, you go to a hotel or restaurant and you're welcome to use their facility. That did not work in Russia as the guards were instructed not to admit strangers to avoid crime problems. Sometimes children, students and other Russians went to the toilet to resolve their tensions and problems. Sadly enough, it could result in fighting.

Religion in the USSR - Revelations of Suppressing Christians

Did you know that the USSR did not sign the Universal Declaration of Human Rights, adopted by the United Nations, which in Article 18 states: "Everyone has the right to freedom of thought, conscience and religion..."

Did you know that Russia did not publish this Universal Declaration and did not make it public till 1989? At the same time, the Soviet Constitution, the Fundamental Law, included a clause about the freedom of religion yet violated it on a daily basis by persecuting, suppressing and destroying Christians in the Communist Russia.

Did you know that the Bible was not available to Russians throughout the Communist period, that people could not buy it in bookstores or borrow it from the libraries, offices or research centers, that the Bible was forbidden fruit, the most secret document in the country?

Did you know there were government agencies at all levels of the Russian Government whose job was to control and suppress Christians in Russia?

Did you know that the accurate number of religious believers and Christians was never disclosed in Communist Russia and became public only after the collapse of the Communist Empire?

Did you know that mandatory courses on atheism were taught at most levels of Soviet schools?

Did you know there were only two functioning Russian Orthodox churches in the city of Odessa with a population more than a million residents and one of them was constantly closed for repair in any given year?

My parents experienced this persecution and suppression and were not allowed to show any of their religious beliefs publicly for fear of being persecuted. As a child I remember going to our village church which was brutally destroyed by the Khrushchev Government in 1962, one of 12,000 Russian Orthodox churches destroyed in the country during that period. The clergy was disorganized and petrified. The Moscow Patriarch praised the Russian government and sanctioned firing the priests. Most religious believers became closet Christians. They had to hide their faith and could not show their love of God. They could not worship publicly; it was not safe. They could have been exposed and imprisoned. A war was declared by the Communist Government against its own people, in which the anti-religious propaganda and the suppressive monster, KGB, had the carte blanche.

The KGB used such repressive methods as registering all religious sects, recruiting clergy men as their agents, tapping the phones of Christians, bugging and surveillance of church offices, infiltration and penetration of parishes, moral defeat, life threats, imprisonment, expulsion and deportation, and the physical destruction of church properties. Such actions are a horrendous legacy that Communists left to the Russians and Christians.

In the 1970s, the exact number of God believers in the USSR was not known. Such statistics were closed and a deep secret. Soviet authorities and the system did not want to encourage Soviet people to know God's word. In the West, very uncertain estimates ranged between 40 and 90 million believers in the USSR. In Odessa, with a population of 1,000,100 citizens, we had two Russian Orthodox churches called cathedral small churches, the Uspensky Assumption Cathedral, one small Polish church, a synagogue (Judaic community) and a monastery.

In the early 1980s, I was on the Board of Examiners of the candidates for guide interpreters at our International Youth Travel Bureau Sputnik. All candidates were tested on several topics: foreign languages, the USSR political system, current events and cultural issues. One of the examiners asked a student how many believers in God there were in the USSR. The student did not know and the session was over. We asked the examiner who was an expert in atheism to give us the answer. He asked a counter question – how many believers did we think there were? Some of us said forty million, others sixty million. The professor answered, "We wish there were less, but we have about hundred million God believers in Russia.

As tour guides we were advised by our bosses and supervisors not to show Western visitors the location of the Odessa synagogue. If I had, it would have cost me my job, my career, and I would be the owner of a "wolf's card," that is, added to the blacklist of the disloyal, those deemed not loyal to the Soviet regime. Another example of a "wolf's card" offense: Two very experienced guide interpreters and good friends of mine from Moldova, were obstructed and punished for their open-mindedness and finally fired by the KGB for arguing with their bosses who were conducting political propaganda training for full time interpreters. A little background: When Stalin took office the Soviets changed Roman letters for the Moldavian dialect into the Cyrillic alphabet for political reasons when they occupied the right bank of the Dniester River territory which nowadays is still a bleeding wound that festers between Russians and Moldavians of the Transdniestrian Republic. One of my friends said publicly that Moldavian was only a *dialect* of the Rumanian language. The other friend said something about "Communist Party involvement" regarding the changing of the alphabet. For those statements, they were both fired and put on black list as they got the "wolf's card."

I did not know the location of the Odessa synagogue until my wife, being Jewish and having the right to emigrate to Israel and decided to take Hebrew courses. Hebrew was an ancient, dead language and was completely outlawed in the USSR. All Jews who tried to learn it before emigrating to Israel were imprisoned. To avoid imprisonment, many Jews took underground Hebrew courses and if discovered, were charged with Anti-Soviet propaganda and put on the black list of the KGB. I saw Hebrew books in 1990 in Moscow, but it was too late because millions of Jews had already immigrated to Israel and different countries the world.

I went to sign up the then my wife, now ex-wife, and myself for Hebrew courses in January 1991 and paid the fee. On the reverse side of the stamped card was printed "Odessa Judaistic Community." The local newspaper, Evening Odessa, did not use the moral Judaistic term but the word "Jewish" instead. In USSR not all Jews were religious, that's why we use different words to be precise. There were only three percent of the Jews that were religious Judaists.

I brought pictures of the other Odessa synagogues that existed before Communists seized power and I showed them to Tsilya, an eighty year old Jewish lady. She couldn't recognize the buildings or recall the locations or identify the locations the synagogues which were destroyed by the Communists.

There is no freedom of worship and religion of a Soviet style. I think I visited the Odessa synagogue once or twice. It was built out of downtown in the forefront of a historically poor and, at that time, industrial district. Americans would call it a depressed area. The area was called Peresup (to pour from one place to another, to pour off, to interfere). It was symbolic that the synagogue was built away from the busy center, away from the financial and commercial buildings.

In the late 1960's, Israeli tourists visited Odessa and tried to distribute some religious literature, such as the Talmud and Tara. They were under constant surveillance by the KGB, were finally seized, arrested, charged with Anti Soviet propaganda and imprisoned. Such cases were numerous. It was a real diplomatic scandal. Some Odessa Jewish residents who had relatives in Israel, the USA and Canada visited Odessa and their relatives.

According to the Soviet Constitution, foreign visitors were not allowed to bring into the USSR any religious books. They were carefully searched by Customs officers when crossing the Soviet border and if found, deprived of the Bible, Torah or any kind of religious books. Ironically, the same USSR Constitution referred to as the fundamental law of the country stated that there was freedom of religion and worship.

You could not enjoy your freedom if you were not allowed to exercise your rights. Odessa has several public libraries, college libraries, and Gorky public library. The largest library had over two million books, but not a single copy of the Bible!

I made friends with an American visitor from France who had a business contract with a Paris hospital. She brought "Russians" by Hedrick Smith to the USSR to read. At the Soviet border Customs House she was carefully searched including all her luggage, belongings, valuables and books. The customs inspector was unhappy with the truthful book; he made an entry in the visitor's passport, according to which she was ordered to bring back that book with her when leaving USSR. She gave me the "Russians" to read and I enjoyed it for the first time as I read it. I returned her book so she would not get in trouble with the Soviet authorities upon departure. Later I advised after my arrival in the USA, for my students to read the book whenever I lectured in United States universities.

The rest of the world did not know, but in the USSR there is a long list of books prohibited, "the black list of books." These books were deemed Anti-Soviet and religious propaganda. Pornography was also included in the "black list." The list was compiled by the KGB and updated every week. Customs control inspections were very tough and would last up to four hours which made Western visitors nauseated and dizzy because there was no air conditioning. In my job, as guide and interpreter, I had to meet delegations, groups and individuals from about one hundred and fifty countries from all over the world. Included on the black list of books were those written by Russian émigrés, former Soviet writers, like Al Solzhenitzyn, VI Nabokov, An Kuznetsov, Aldanov, VI Maksimov and Svetlana Alilueva, Stalin's daughter. They knew the USSR well and gave truthful pictures of life there. The Soviet propaganda machine did not want the truth. The customs officer on duty would go into the office while searching a Western visitor and check to see if a book was on the black list. If it was, he would keep the book for himself and for his coworkers or bosses.

Anti-Semitism in the USSR and in Eastern Europe

"The true emancipation of the Jews of Eastern Europe will come only with the emancipation of the non-Jews from the role of oppressor, from the psychology of persecutor." This quote is from the Annual Report of the Executive Committee of the American Jewish Committee at its 13th annual meeting, October 19, 1919, quoted in *American Jewish Year Book 1920-1921.*"

"Anti-Semitism is the longest-running, most widely adopted social pathology in history." Rabbi Irving Greenberg, author, scholar, and founder of CLAL, quoted in the *"Jewish Week,"* March 12, 1992.

As a Jewish lady Svetlana, (Sveta, my wife at that time since 1976 and, now ex-wife) and our family were eligible to apply for Israeli permanent residence visa status because Sveta had a relative, a first cousin living in Israel. We considered the option of immigrating to Israel until I met our sponsors. There was a big Jewish community in the USSR, mostly in big cities of Moscow, Leningrad, Kiev, Riga, Vilnius and Odessa too.

I visited some of my fellow Jewish writers when I happened to be on business trips in major cities. There was much talk about emigration out of the USSR. We were constantly searching for ways to get out of the USSR legally. The Soviet Jewish community was a very well-informed, supportive community and stayed in touch with each other and shared information about the latest activities and measures by notorious Soviet authorities as to visas for Soviet Jews. We talked at home with the members of our immediate and extended families and

64

relatives on Sveta's side about many different topics: Anti-Semitism, OVIR, refusiniks, visa denials, KGB traps, manipulations, OVIR graduates releaseniks, the suppression of human rights of the Jewish community in the USSR, imprisonment, Siberian exile which was a long, long journey with lots of tribulations, harassments, death threats, trials, stress, disappointments and losses in the families. There were protests and demonstrations at KGB headquarters on Lubyanka in Moscow. There was use of psychiatric hospitals to imprison and suppress Jewish dissidents and protestors and to deny Jews Soviet exit visas. Their correspondence was intercepted and destroyed. There was humiliation and the use of punitive medication.

We knew who were refusniks, mainly Soviet Jews who were denied Soviet exit visas to go and live in Israel or other Western countries. Nevertheless, who were the releasniks? I bet you have not heard about them. Releasniks were graduates of OVIR. After many years of mental and physical torture and denial of Soviet exit visas, and due to the pressure of the international human rights watch groups, finally OVIR granted exit permits and decided to release Russian Jewish citizens and let them go to the Western host countries. These citizens were called "Releasniks."

The names of Jewish dissidents and other prisoners of conscience, like Nathan Shcharanskiy, Iosif Brodsky, Alexander Ginsburg, Andrey Amalrik, Vladimir Bukovsky, Alexander Ginsburg, Andrey Siniavsky, Yury Daniel, and Vasiliy Axionov were the topics of daily news in the Jewish community, but not in the official Soviet press with its draconian, brutal censorship. The Soviet media, the KGB and the official Soviet establishment tried to keep hush-shush and mum about the real situation and truth about Jewish dissidents and imposed cruel restrictions and sanctions both on and against the dissidents, foreign correspondents and even their family members and relatives.

Sveta, her family, and I felt the tension daily, everywhere, starting in the early morning when we were at our high-rise apartment building being greeted by the plumber whose family resided underneath our apartment on the first floor. He would give us a dirty look and start an argument stating that our baby was crying during the night hours and it disturbed their sleep. Very often he would come upstairs and knock on our door late at night and harass us saying he could hear Sveta's grandmother talking and her voice was bothering their child through the wall. Years passed by, their daughter grew up and she followed in her mother's and father's footsteps and on many occasions she would initiate a war of words without any grounds, just because she had a bad dream or got up on the wrong side of the bed.

My day continued by taking the public street car where I could hear some passengers loudly discussing the latest news about dissidents' imprisonment and calling them derogatory, hateful names: "Jidos" and "kinky." Those derogatory, hateful, hostile names were used daily in the USSR, both by ordinary, common people, the rank and file, and by the brass in the executive and corporate community (they whispered them not to be heard). Some of the abusers would use those names in a relaxed manner without caring if there were any Jews near them or without any fear of being punished. Guess what? The abusers were not punished, they were not taken to the Soviet court system to penalize them and stop the anti-Semitism, humiliation and abuse. I do not remember reading reports of taking such abusers to court for using anti-Semitic slurs which shows how deep rooted, infectious, contagious, unpunished and un-punishable was anti-Semitism in Communist Russia and how unjust the Soviet justice system.

We discussed the above numerous topics with my family, mainly at our apartment in Odessa with Sveta and at her relatives' houses. Our apartment, we were sure, was bugged by the KGB because of the nature of my work. I was a full-time guide-interpreter working with various tour delegations from all over the world. There were only a few linguists in Odessa in positions like mine, which is why we were closely supervised by the KGB and which is why we were sure that our phone was wiretapped and our apartment bugged. The Soviet Government did not spare money for highly sophisticated technology to spy on its own citizens, although it did not care at all about basic needs of its population. Other reasons for our apartment being bugged and our phone tapped was because Sveta is Jewish and she had several relatives who emigrated to Israel. I was very mobile because of my work. I traveled a lot around the USSR and met many people, and I was a published freelance writer and knew many writers around the USSR. Such people of my background and interest, accomplishments were always of interest to and under surveillance of the KGB. It was not safe to meet or stay in touch with Soviet Jewish dissidents, but the word of mouth spread fast, especially in the tightly-enclosed Jewish community.

66

Our fight with OVIR, the Regional Committee on Foreign Relations, and the KGB was primarily over my ethnicity and background, my children, their Jewish ethnicity and background, their biological mother's Jewish ethnicity and persecution because of Anti-Semitism, pogroms, Pamyat, and anti-Semitic organizations in Russia in late 1980s and later. Anti-Semitism is in the blood of many Russians and other ethnic groups of the former USSR and has been there for many centuries. Such terms as OVIR, refusnik, otkaznik, pogrom, dissidents, dissenters are closely and easily associated with Jews in the USSR and with most respected Jews all over the world: Nathan Shcharanskiy, Iosif Brodsky, Alexander Ginsburg, Andrey Amalrik, and Vasiliy Axionov.

OVIR—Russian for notorious Otdel Viz I Registrazii, the Visa and Registration Department of the USSR's Interior Ministry (analog to the National Federal Police Force Department) in charge of scanning, screening, vetting, investigation, issuance, vetting, approval, denial, rejection of the visas, entry visas, exit visas, exit permits, visas to Soviet citizens and foreigners, notorious for obstructing the justice and multiple violations of international human rights including but not limited to: the rights to passage, travel abroad, discrimination, Anti-Semitism, and freedom of speech.

Surely you have heard about the many hundreds of years of history of Russian immigration, Russians immigrating, escaping from anti-Semitism and pogroms, defecting and desperately seeking political asylum or refuge in other countries of the world. One intellectual with an ultra chauvinist mindset advised Russian immigrants in the whole world: "Russians Must Stay and Live in Russia." He certainly heard and read about the United Nations Universal Declaration of Human Rights adopted in 1948, but not ratified by the USSR during the Soviet period 1917-1991, because the USSR knew it would be in big-big trouble with the international laws and human rights issues if it signed the Declaration, which, by the way, Mr. Nechuev states, it is the right of a citizen to take a domicile and live in any country of the world.

Maya Plisetskaya is one of the best examples of ethnic Jews and was a great success story in USSR. Although there were many such examples there, Maya Plisetskaya was a top, world class Bolshoi Theater (Moscow) ballerina and winner of prestigious awards, she danced on all the most renowned stages of the world after she joined the Bolshoi in 1943. She was born into a Jewish family of eleven children. Her grandfather was a dentist. Students and soldiers were offered free of charge dental services at his office. Two of her children, Sulamif and Assaf, become ballet dancers also. Sulamif was Russia's champion in swimming and Assaf was a great soccer player. In the ballet, "Swan Lake," Maya Plisetskaya's swan dance was considered the best in the world. Her mother, Rahil Rah was a famous movie actress.

TV Comes to Russia

In the second half of the 1960's, TV sets were bought by the local residents in my community. My daddy's brother's son Milyu, or Mikhail, was among the first in the village to buy a TV set. His TV set had a tall, about seven to twelve meters high antenna like a pole. It was a fantasy land, a dreamland, a wonderland when we first experienced the TV appearance in our community. We would go to his house, crowd the living room where the TV was, and the small hallway next to the living room. My memories of the TV shows and programs are of those of the Rumanian TV station and programs from Bucharest. We had time to watch TV shows mainly in the evening and night time. It was a revolution for our minds and mentality. We typically watched folk music, dance shows, and movies. Rumanian was not taught at the school in my village, but the older generation of my parents' ages lived under Rumanian monarchy ruling. They knew and spoke Rumanian. They used the Rumanian language to joke, to cuss, to speak privately so, the kids, could not understand their conversations. Some of the adult men's jokes were in Rumanian about women or about sex. Some of the movies were Rumanian, broadcast from Romania; others were Western or US-made. TV programs also included sports broadcasts like soccer, basketball, and tennis. Most of those were international competitions. Our village, at that time in the sixties, was outside the reach of the Soviet National TV, known in the West as Moscow Television.

April 1986 Chernobyl Nuclear Disaster

USSR's national tragedy and major environmental crisis of nuclear fallout at the Chernobyl nuclear power plant happened on April 26, 1986. Chernobyl is less than a hundred kilometers from Kiev, the Ukraine's major city and about four hundred kilometers away from

Odessa, the city where my sons, my ex-wife, and I lived as an adult. The graphite core during the test of its functions at the Reactor Unit #4 of the nuclear plant caught fire and burned for ten days. Nine tons of fuel went into the fallout cloud, of which one ton fell back on the site, while the rest was blown away by the wind toward Western European countries, thus increasing the radiation level.

The Soviet authorities kept silence until August 21, 1986, at a news conference during which six managers were given jail sentences. Thirty one staff members were killed in the explosion; one died fighting the fire; over two hundred suffered from acute radiation exposure; 135,000 people were evacuated from the surrounding areas for a certain period. I do remember the immediate assistance and humanitarian aid that was immediately dispatched to the USSR to help with the nuclear disaster. Dr. Robert Gale from the United States arrived to help counsel Soviet experts on how to handle the tragedy. His help was greatly appreciated by the Soviet people and the officials. I have two personal journals that I kept while in the USSR, from 1984 until our departure from Russia in 1991. Like all other Soviet people, I was not aware of the Chernobyl nuclear accident and kept going to work, walking with my family to the beach, swimming in the Black Sea, visiting our relatives, spending time outside, giving city tours to Soviet and foreign tourist groups including a group from the United States. The Soviet Government kept mum, concealed and delayed all information related to the tragedy. Luckily, my knowledge of foreign languages (English, German, Rumanian, Bulgarian, Serbo-Croatian and French) came to my rescue using our short-wave radio set. At night I could tune to Western radio stations, Voice of America, Radio Liberty and Radio Free Europe to get the truth about the nuclear accident and updates on the Chernobyl nuclear reactor, plant rescue and repair. I saw the contaminated streets and cities of the Ukraine and how the water tank trucks in Odessa sprayed streets and sidewalks with water which was like a Band-Aid on a deadly wound. I saw government employees walking on the sidewalks in Odessa, in the Arkadya beach area, with hand-held, human size height tools pointed to the ground, that they claimed to be Geiger counters to measure radiation levels. Although the radiation level was way too high, Soviet Government did not reveal to the Soviet people its highly dangerous level and ignored requests from Western governments to disclose the truth about the extent of the tragedy and its consequences because the Soviet authorities did not want to cooperate and to be held liable. I do remember well that we, full-time guide-interpreters working in the travel industry were horrified and scared to go on business trips after the Chernobyl tragedy, to host groups and to visit Kiev, which was one the major and favorite destinations on the itineraries of the majority of tourist groups both from the Western and other countries of the world. Luckily, my tour assignments to Kiev were cancelled due to the Chernobyl tragedy, the Soviet tourist industry suffered very significant losses of revenues and its image never regain consciousness.

Guide-Interpreter at Reny International Seamen's Club

"Success is not final. Failure is not final. It is the courage to continue that counts."

Sir Winston Churchill

"Success stops when you do." Unknown

I got an honorable discharge from the Soviet Army, also called the Red Army in the West, in December 1975, after serving one year as a private. Conscription was mandated in Russia and the adult males had to serve two years in the army and three in the navy.

In the same month I got a brief stint as a full time temporary news reporter for the city newspaper "Sovetskiy Izmail" in the city of Izmail, Odessa Oblast, Ukraine, USSR. That was my college city and where my would-be wife, Svetlana Postolovskaya, now ex-wife, was finishing her senior year at Izmail State Teachers' Training College, also my alma mater. After my reporter's stint, I got a full time job in Reny, Odessa Oblast, Ukraine. Reny is a small port city, by Soviet standard, on the Danube River across from Romania. After an interview with the General Manager, I started my employment with Reny International Seamen's Club in January 1976, that lasted through November 1976. Sveta and I had married in January 1976. The Reny Club was a type of Community Activity Center which offered a variety of activities with entertainment and a lot of Soviet communist propaganda lecturing and talking to the ships crews and their families: sailors, seamen, captains, first mates, and second mates of the ships. The crews came from different countries of the world, but mainly from the Danube River basin and Mediterranean, Black Sea countries: Bulgaria, Romania, Yugoslavia, Hungary, Poland, Czechoslovakia, Austria, F.R.G. (the Federal Republic of Germany), Greece and Italy. Per Soviet Government regulations, those delegations were divided into "Top Priority," or, as they were called in Russian, "Special Attention" groups, i.e., VIPs or very important persons who came from Western, capitalist countries. A second category of ordinary delegations that dominated our visitors' list came from the Soviet bloc satellite socialist countries. Since the Western delegations were of special interest and special importance to Soviet authorities, we were instructed to serve them better, do our very best, pay special attention to the delegations from the Western countries, be very considerate and polite, watch our language and be cautious of our contacts with such groups. Very often the KGB debriefed or interviewed us afterward and asked specific questions related to such groups. This was true also when I got my job as the full time guide-interpreter with IYTB "Sputnik" in the Odessa local office.

At the Reny Club we offered different activities: a hard currency (Western currency) bar with food and snacks mainly and a library which gave away books in several foreign languages, including English, French, Hungarian and German. We also had a lounge, music, dance parties, entertainment mainly related to Soviet celebrations like New Year, Victory Day (the 9th of May), Bolshevik Revolution Day, visiting shows, modern variety and music shows. I remember one of the shows by Mariya Kodriyanu from Moldavia. The Club arranged visits to local middle or high schools, the Pioneer Palace, i.e. the Boy Scouts center. The Club offered presentations and lectures by Soviet speakers especially trained and well prepared to face and debate diverse foreign audiences from various countries of the world, including Western countries, and defend the Soviet Marxist-Leninist tenets and doctrines. The presentations included current situations, world and national affairs, history, official Soviet opinions on international affairs and developments: Communist Party of the USSR, Party congress guidelines, SALT, the strategic arms limitations treaty, nuclear weapons negotiations, WWII and cold war issues. These were pretty boring topics and presentations in most cases. Definitely, like IYTB "Sputnik," Reny International Seamen's Club was completely controlled by the KGB. Guide-interpreters were debriefed and questioned by KGB officers about the contents of meetings and conversations we had with the visiting groups.

The Club had so-called "Aktiv" (included in the Glossary of Soviet speak) analogue in American English for the pool of volunteers, which stands in Russian for a group of well screened, vetted, scrutinized, instructed and trained individuals who passed all types of background and criminal checks by the KGB: free-lance interpreters, translators, activists, volunteers, young people, mainly girls, as was the case with our Club, who were trained to host, deal and debate with foreign, visiting guests. No doubt, since they were well-screened by the KGB, they were all considered to be patriots and loyal to the Communist party and its ideology, or at least in their words and deeds. In order to prove their loyalty some or most of the women had specific assignments to approach certain foreigners, especially from Western countries and get them involved in certain activities, operations, provocations, including "honey traps", i.e. sex traps and *sexpioanage* involving guests and visitors in parties with an abundance of alcohol, then taking them to a hotel or private apartment, luring them into intimate encounters and having sex. The "Aktiv" people were the Soviet Communist ideological SWAT team.

The hard currency bar at Reny Club was actually run by assistant manager's wife, a bartender, who was always there drinking at the guests' expense and generosity. It was very convenient for the KGB to have a family, and unusual for Soviet employment practices simply you did not see husband and wife working together at such a sensitive work place with only a few employees (ten approximately at the Club) dealing daily with foreign visitors from a wide variety of countries, as the deputy general manager of the Club and his wife serving and waiting on the guests. I do not remember her background, but she was very possessive, bossy and probably had some linguistic training, so she could understand foreign visitors' conversations and actually report them to the KGB. I think she spoke Romanian, the Moldavian dialect of it. She was skillfully supported by her husband who spent most of his Reny Club career in the hard currency bar drinking very expensive alcohol at the expense of kind and welcoming foreign guests. Assistant General Manager's background was in linguistics; I think he graduated from Izmail State Teachers' Training College and majored in French, maybe minored in English and spoke several languages as I am not certain. He seemed to be very confident and good communicator when dealing with the foreign visitors. As a duet, he and his wife made a next to perfect couple to entertain the guests, drinking, cutting up with them and then conveniently reporting to the KGB which was probably part and condition of their employment.

It was normal practice for many Soviet organizations, mainly those involved in hospitality and tourism, to ask visiting delegations to write down their impressions of their stay in the USSR on a piece of paper, on an approved form with the company letterhead. Special questionnaires asked tour delegation leaders to evaluate food, customer service, transportation, hotel accommodations, in-country host guide-interpreters' performance, i.e., his/her foreign language skills, personal job performance, social activities, programs, visits, and friendship meetings. The higher the evaluation was, especially by Western delegations, the better were the records of the host travel agency or in this case, the Reny Club Community Center, and the more incentives the staff got. To both the management and its support staff, a good evaluation might mean a bonus or two during the year, a promotion, a good to excellent performance evaluation or better job opportunities. So, we guide-interpreters made sure we gave those questionnaires to the visiting delegations leaders and got them back completed before they left town. Having negative evaluations listed on such forms could have severe consequences for us and the entire office.

Our Club's staff was small by Soviet standards: the general manager, his VP, or deputy general manager, accountant, facility manager, four full-time-guide interpreters, like myself, speaking German, English, Rumanian, Bulgarian, and other languages. We had also "aktiv" which was not officially on the Club's payroll.

That was the name of the game. Remember, Soviet Premier N. Khrushchev: "We will bury you!" when he was tapping with his dirty shoe at the U.N.O. session table? The USSR was always in rivalry with the West and to have compliments, admissions and approval of visitors from Western countries in writing was a victory for the Soviets and a loss for Westerners in the eyes of Soviet propaganda. Here are a few quotes from John Gunther's book Inside Russia Today, published by Harper's in 1957. Gunther was an American who traveled a lot around the world, knew much about various countries and had first-hand knowledge about Russia:

"If Russians were permitted to travel indiscriminately, they would see what the rest of the world is like, realize how appallingly low their own standard of living is by comparison and become disgruntled. Soviet officials going abroad and members of various scientific and cultural exchange groups are carefully handpicked."

"Russians realize perfectly well that to let in (foreign) tourists without a limit is a risk. Foreign (especially, Western) tourists bring fresh air from the world outside, which can be dangerous... A tourist is a valuable article of export...."

Although J. Gunther's remarks were written many years ago, they are true and very relevant to the period of my life in the USSR. I wrote in this book before I read J. Gunther's notes about Western tourists being and bringing fresh air from the free, Western world. As you will see in another chapter of this book, I share my great experience of having the special privilege to be the guide-interpreter and to host different delegations and tourist groups from all over the world. Western and other foreign tourists were not only fresh air to me, but also conduits and ambassadors of the free world, pioneers of liberties, freedoms and of a different, special lifestyle. The people I met from all over the Western world instilled in me the hope that one day my family and I could make it out of the Soviet Iron Curtain hell and find ourselves in "the land of opportunity" and pursue our own American dream in a free world and enjoy freedoms like other Americans. Most of the Soviet people did not have such a privilege like myself as to work and host Western and other foreign visiting delegations. On the contrary, Soviet secret police severely guarded Russians from any types of contacts or communications whether casual, official, impromptu, spontaneous or just on the spot with visiting foreign delegations, especially from Western countries. Because it was a closed Soviet Iron Curtain society and most Western powers, per Soviet military doctrine, were the USSR's official adversaries, or more simply put our enemies.

Guide-Interpreter at International Youth Travel Bureau "Sputnik"

After I resigned from the Reny International Seamen's Club in November 1976, I found a new job in Odessa when I moved to live with Sveta, her grandmother and her grandmother's sister.

I started working for Sputnik in Odessa. There were cases at our office in Odessa IYTB "Sputnik" when our big-mouth dispatcher was not happy with an evaluation and some comments that Western group leaders provided to our office. When this happened, she held urgent peace-negotiation talks and made the tour delegation leader rewrite the responses to our questionnaire, remove negative comments and leave only positive, boastful remarks e.g., the food that was not actually tasty and healthy, but was the only food the host city could offer at that time, or comments about our warm Odessa hospitality. Much was at stake and she did not want any trouble, or to jeopardize her job as actually she was an expert in twisting hands and minds too when dealing with foreign delegations. She held a desk job, spoke poor English and never mastered it, but she was loyal to the Communist system, was vetted and approved by the KGB as she travelled several times as the interpreter for Soviet tourist groups traveling to Western countries. Sometimes the local, city and regional newspapers published a selection of the best, most complimentary remarks, notes and comments provided by visiting Western tourist leaders and they served as very important propaganda tools. It meant a lot to have compliments, positive and welcoming remarks from but the visiting Western citizens and delegation leaders, stating that they were delighted and pleased with Soviet hospitality, accommodations, customer service, and actually and ultimately, the Soviet way of life, which was a propaganda trick used often.

The title of my full-time position was guide-interpreter with the International Youth Travel Bureau "Sputnik" in Odessa, Ukraine. I got the job due to my educational background, skill sets, extensive linguistics skills, writing skills as a free-lance writer, lexicographer's skills and language expertise, extensive experience, translation and interpretation skills, general knowledge, and credentials. My detailed experience and expertise at that time looked like this: I graduated from the college, majoring in English and a minor in French. I studied Latin, German, Serbo-Croatian at the college and attended language courses at local night schools and foreign language classes, seminars and presentations in

Izmail, Odessa, and Kiev, national and international IYT Bureau "Sputnik" conventions, something that may be called CLE-Continued Linguistic Education.

It was real luck to find that job so that I could reunite with my then-wife, now ex-wife, Sveta, and live with her and her grandma and aunt in Odessa. The office for my new job with Sputnik in late 1976 was located in Odessa which by the Black Sea. Our travel service, "Sputnik," was named after the world's first Soviet artificial satellite, "Sputnik," that orbited the earth many times and set up the tone of the US-USSR rivalry in space exploration.

First, Bulgarian is my mother tongue. Russian was the native language of Big Brother, Big Government and the official language of the Soviet Union. Ukrainian, my second native language, is that of the Smaller Big Brother, called Small Russian, "Malorussky" language, Ukrainians being called "Malorossy," "Small Russians; Russians, Minor" in Russian. Where I was born most of the official business and document handling, keeping records, and recording the official legal documents in Ukraine were handled in two languages Russian and Ukrainian.

The USSR's International Youth Travel Bureau "Sputnik" was founded in 1957, as a youth travel service mainly to serve Russian school students, the school staff and faculty members, their teachers and school personnel mainly from the USSR. Later its operations expanded and served both the national youth tourist groups from the USSR and foreign groups from all over the world. IYTB "Sputnik" was a competitor, to a certain degree, of the Soviet Trade Union Travel Bureau Service which operated mainly in the USSR. "Sputink" was to a lesser degree a rival "Intourist" Travel Service, a notorious, big-wig travel service tailored to Western and foreign tourists. "Intourist" specialized mainly in hosting a huge variety of foreign delegations, mainly Western, including high-level, top officials, top level executives and top military brass that covers also bilateral, governmental, official dignitaries, royalty, military, law enforcement agency delegations and "special attention" delegations called in Russian lingo, "gruppi osobogo vnimaniya," which can very loosely be translated as VIP delegations.

International Youth Travel Bureau "Sputnik had branches, affiliates, divisions, local and regional offices in major cities of the USSR, typically, in the capital cities, major tourist centers, destinations or historic landmarks. Leningrad (now St. Petersburg), Kiev, Odessa, Vilnius, Tallinn, Riga, Rostov-on-Don, Yerevan, Tbilisi and Tashkent. The Central Office of the International Youth Travel Bureau "Sputnik," was definitely in Big Brother's Big Government's major city, the heart of the Soviet Empire, the ancient city, the heart of matushka-Rossiya (mother-Russia) Moscow. Apart from the "Sputnik" Central Office, Moscow hosted its own city branch office of the International Youth Travel Bureau "Sputnik" which was, by all means, measures and standards, the largest in the nation, the most efficient and the most powerful "Sputnik" office in the USSR. Why? Because Moscow was the largest USSR city, a great historic, social and geopolitical hub of the Soviet bloc countries, the center of international tourism, diplomacy and politics, often frequented by foreign tourists, the brain of the mysterious and mystique "matushka-Rossiya" (mother-Russia). Moscow typically was included most itineraries of tourist groups and delegations, which is why the city was at all times busy, overcrowded and over-packed. Long, long lines were the typical scene there.

  The low level of Soviet customer service and the high level of Soviet red tape bureaucracy were notorious all over the world. These factors caused serious problems servicing tourist delegations and resulted in offering poor service quality. I witnessed both and beyond that. Here are illustrative examples of outrageously poor customer service and Soviet red-red Red Tape: as in-country host guide-interpreter I had many responsibilities and duties, some of them unimaginable and impossible. My work day consisted, not of nine to ten hours, but more like fourteen to twenty four hours per day for three hundred and fifty two days per year. When arriving in Moscow and bringing a group, I had to go to the downtown Moscow City "Sputnik" office to secure a voucher check book with vouchers to feed the group, i.e. to write the checks to pay restaurants and museums for the foreign tourist groups I led. Most of the tourist bus drivers would not drive from Red Square parking to the Moscow City downtown "Sputnik" office, saying they, drivers, are not allowed to park there, because there was no designated parking space for the "Sputnik" group buses, which was true. We, the guide-interpreters, were ordered by local Moscow City office dispatchers to leave the group in the Red Square area, which might have been half a mile or more of a walk, or in the museum parking lot and rush to the downtown "Spuntik" office. It was a long walk to the Moscow city office and there was a line to wait and to do formalities there, to get to the accounting department, to find the right person, who was often not at his/her desk, but somewhere else either smoking, chatting, or drinking alcohol something (depending on the time of the day). Closer to the dispatcher's office, you could feel the alcohol and sweat coming out of that small room which reminded me more of horse stables as a typical Soviet scene, make it plural scenes. My staunch impressions of the Moscow City "Sputnik" personnel and the Moscow-based "Sputnik" dispatchers service and their very small personnel was that they were not helpful, but they were arrogant, disrespectful, inept, incompetent, unqualified and not mindful of their jobs; the list goes on. I knew personally a few dispatchers at the Moscow "Sputnik" office, stationed at "Molodyozhnaya" and "Orlyonok" hotels, who graduated from prestigious colleges, universities or institutes, like the Moscow Institute of Foreign Languages, the Moscow Institute of Foreign Translators and Interpreters, MGIMO (Russian for: Moskovskiy Gosudarstvenniy Institut Mezhdunarodnih Otnosheniy, the Moscow State University for International Relations that trained many Soviet diplomats, many of whom were recruited by the KGB, trained and posted in foreign countries, including the West: USA, U.K., Great Britain, Canada, Germany, Italy, France, or Japan. One may ask: what is the point of graduating from such very prestigious Soviet colleges and then to be sitting as a desk jockey as a pack rat in a small, busy dispatcher's office of a youth travel service? Good question. My possible answers: 1. That graduate was recruited by the KGB and posted there at the "Sputnik" office with particular (temporary) assignments and jobs, which changed every day, depending on the KGB operatives' needs as happened often. It is possible that it was an entry KGB undercover position, not significant, but a good launching pad for future promotions and career jumps. That graduate was in the waiting period till his assignment or turn came to be appointed to a better position, hopefully abroad, his/her preference, number one choice would be definitely a Western country as every Soviet citizen dreamed about getting out 2. That graduate did not have enough pull, connections in higher-ups, "blat," (Russian for clout, power or influence) you are getting my point. 3. That graduate (the 'Sputnik" dispatcher) was a loser and could not get a better job as of that time, but maybe was still searching for a better one to utilize his linguistic training. 4. That graduate did not have an influential Communist daddy, uncle, or father-in-law high up in the

Soviet, Moscow-based Communist hierarchy. 5. Actually, some of those dispatchers were back home from postings overseas, possibly waiting for a new assignment or got demoted and were between the jobs. There were many possible scenarios in that corrupt, very corrupt, Soviet society.

Apart from all that, "Sputnik" dispatchers were our bosses and they had reporting authority, the power to report on us, which they did use, often abused, loosely. The reporting power was actually a punitive measure, a license to steal, to false report, to create a penalty. The reporting power was designed to keep "Sputnik" guide-interpreters in fear and constant obedience, not to voice their opinions or protests related to the "Sputnik" travel service. If the dispatcher did not like an out-of-town guide-interpreter, or that interpreter did not want to have sex with that dispatcher (most of dispatchers were males and most of my full-time and part-time guide-interpreter friends were females), then the dispatcher could send a slander, a complaint to the "Sputnik" Central office, copying the home office on the slanderous report, informing the bosses that the guide did something, like: the guide was always late for regular tour group meals, or, the guide did not check the tour program schedule every evening with dispatcher for potential changes for the next day, which miraculously and conveniently for the dispatcher, always happened at around midnight, the perfect time for the dispatcher's cup of coffee mixed with brandy and a cigar with a pretty girl, a guide-interpreter in a private room; or the guide's conduct was too casual with a Western tourist group, which was unacceptable by the "Sputnik" policy and KGB rules; a dispatcher's suspicion of intimate relations between the guide and the foreign tourist. The list was never ending, ever-lasting.

One more example of poor customer service and Soviet Red Tape bureaucracy happened at the "Molodyozhnaya" hotel which was built specifically for guests of the XXII Summer World Olympic Games in Moscow. It had many guests, which was a normal scene during the daytime as the tourist buses and coaches took all parking lot spaces and other buses assigned to tourist groups staying at the same "Molodyozhnaya" hotel had to drive away and search for available space to park, which typically was a huge distance away from the hotel. The "Sputnik" office dispatcher and we interpreters were not informed either of the whereabouts of the bus or the bus driver. This was the norm. One more vintage example: You, the in-country host guide-interpreter, bring your lovely tourist group to the huge Tourist Complex compound of the ten hotel high-rise buildings, owned by the Soviet trade union travel service, in northern part of Moscow, next to famous VDNKH, USSR's National Economy Expo and your group was staying at one of these hotels. However as their guide and interpreter you do not know where to go because nobody told you that, or gave you the map of the complex (no GPS or satellite maps at that time) the instructions, or even a guide book. There were no cell phones, mobile phones, pagers, or walkie-talkies in 1970's and 1980's in the USSR for us. You are lost, your bus driver is of no help, you try to find the public phone in that pitch darkness. Finally you walk into one of the hotel lobbies and the typical Russian receptionist with sloppy make-up "kindly," "politely," does not allow you use the phone oh no, you are not their employee, you are stranger to them even though your tourist group was staying at the hotel. Oh, sir, so sorry, let me check—no, your group is not staying here. Good bye. No phone for you. Good luck, be good, get out of my hotel like now out, or I will call the police. Finally, by miracle, I managed to find the public phone outside somewhere next to some bushes. It is raining cats and dogs and there is a long line waiting for that phone and everybody in line ahead of me is begging for my coins to make a phone call. When I stopped giving away my change then the locals start to threaten me, which is normal for that darkness Soviet period. Luckily, my colleague from the "Sputnik" office in Kishinev, Moldavia sees me in the line to the phone booth and helps me to make that magic call to the smoke shop of the "Sputnik" dispatcher office. (yes, actually it was always packed with a thick, poisonous smoke as it was indeed a smoke shop, that is my staunch impression.) I am certain many will confirm it.

Yet another example of poor customer service and Soviet Red Tape: imagine your foreign tourist group member, a tourist got a health emergency and you are the jack of all trades. You need to help that tourist as it's your duty with no questions asked. The local "Sputnik" office was not flexible as the whole group of thirty to forty plus tourists (depending on the contract) will have to wait in the bus, outside the bus and smoke (if any smokers), go to the bar, throw Frisbee, throw a ball, play cards, or just be deadly bored while the interpreter helps the tourist either in the hotel first aid office or drop him at the doctor's office then the whole day tour program is messed up, the whole group suffered. It was an emergency, no doubt, but the local "Sputnik" office was not in a position typically to provide help and assign local qualified, approved

80

and accredited guide-interpreter to accompany and assist the tourist with his/her health emergency problem. That was the way things were done in that hospitality industry, in Russia-c'est la vie.

IYTB "Sputnik" maintained business relations with foreign partners and competitor the Soviet satellite socialist camp countries East European countries: "Orbita" in Bulgaria, in GDR, German Democratic Republic, "Juventus" in Poland, Hungary, Rumania, Czechoslovakia, Cuba, Yugoslavia, with Western countries, including YMCA tourist delegations. We guide-interpreters had several international conventions, typically bilateral. In my case, I remember the conference in Odessa between the USSR's "Sputnik" and Bulgarian "Orbita" Youth Travel Service. The bilateral international conference was saddened by the fact that the plane with several members of the USSR's "Sputnik" Central Office scheduled to participate in that conference, crashed during takeoff at the Moscow-Vnukovo domestic flights airport.. Our boss, the general manager of the Odessa "Sputnik" local office was in Moscow, had the ticket to the same flight, but the fate did him a favor as he was late for that flight and that saved his life. At such international conventions, including bilateral reports were delivered and discussions were held how to improve the customer service, hospitality industry, accommodations, food, and meals quality. I do not believe we succeeded and we did not reach our goals. We had one big problem as there was no competition, no free enterprise, no entrepreneurship, it was also managed, run and mismanaged by the Soviet government.

The "Sputnik" Brotherhood and Sisterhood

I would like to share some great memories of my association and affiliation with The International Youth Travel Bureau "Sputnik," IYTB "Sputnik," the brotherhood and sisterhood of guide-interpreters that I experienced while working as a full-time accredited and certified guide-interpreter for the Odessa branch of "Sputnik." Since Soviet colleges, higher education establishments did not have and were not allowed to have sororities and fraternities, my way to call my affiliations with "Sputnik" guide–interpreters a brotherhood and sisterhood. By that I mean we were like brothers and sisters to each other. It was very special and close bond. The majority of my colleagues at that time were women. For example, in the Odessa branch of "Sputnik" we had only three full-time male interpreters, including myself. Most of my colleagues were well-accomplished professionals, well-trained linguists, translators and interpreters, witty, creative and inventive. They went through rigid language training programs, had unique linguistic experience, including visiting foreign countries or even being posted overseas under different circumstances. We all had to go through a tough, competitive job selection and screening process before being hired full-time or part-time to serve as in-country hosts and guide-interpreters. "Sputnik" had a small percentage of full-time students, professionals, college professors, instructors and teachers whom we trained to work as part-time guide-interpreters. Many of the colleagues with whom I was lucky to work with on many projects and tours, graduated from prestigious colleges, such as Moscow State University, Leningrad State University, Kiev State University, Odessa State University which were top of the line schools, the best education one can get. We shared the "bread and salt," the dramas and comedies of our hard jobs, helping each other survive in the notorious Soviet hospitality industry and doing the best jobs we could.

We shared the tools of the trade, supporting and encouraging each other. Most of us were multilingual interpreters and spoke several languages such as English, Polish, German, Spanish, French, Italian, Rumanian, Bulgarian, and Serbo-Croatian (in this country it is considered to be two languages, I think due to the collapse of Yugoslavia and ethnic issues there). Those were the major languages of groups we encountered when working, touring and hosting foreign delegations from different countries of the world. I was lucky to have been born in a multi-ethnic community where several languages were spoken and languages come naturally to me. Bulgarian is my mother tongue. Moldavian, a dialect of Romanian, was widely spoken by the people of my parents' generation in our village and in Moldavia. My major languages of operation were English, Bulgarian; somewhat less often I used the Serbo-Croatian language when hosting foreign tourist delegations. That was not the case with my colleagues at Sputnik brotherhood/sisterhood as they had to study for years in colleges and become book smart, which they did successfully.

I cannot help but tell you that it was most typical picture to see a Sputnik guide-interpreter smiling and laughing, being cheerful, joking and optimistic for the most of his/her day; actually, that was our normal lifestyle. Where did we get that? Who taught us to do that since Soviet people were considered to be sad and gloomy, as described by Western visitors. Which behavior was true? Who instilled in us that optimism? Maybe we learned it from our patrons, or from Westerners and other tourists? We were good students and listeners, for sure. It was normal to see a Sputnik guide-interpreter with a shoulder bag full of books and multilingual dictionaries to keep up with his/her job and latest trends in her profession. You could see my colleagues riding in tour bus coaches not wasting their time, but looking through and reviewing a bilingual Russian-English glossary of terms, a vocabulary of the museums, such as the Hermitage, that their group was going to visit.

We, guide-interpreters, were not spared the cruelty of the Soviet hospitality tourist industry. I am aware of cases when my colleagues and I, on many occasions, had to wait for hours and hours in lobbies of hotels, typically in Moscow and other big cities (Leningrad and Kiev) during busy days and hours, which was seven days a week and around the clock in the USSR, until we the guide-interpreters got our hotel rooms which we typically shared either with other guide-interpreters or even a Soviet tourist. As a courtesy, our Sputnik sisterhood/brotherhood co-workers would let the waiting guide-interpreter come to his or her hotel room, if you have already been staying at the same hotel and got a room due to your earlier arrival.

To my knowledge and it is my observation, there was no casual or any type of sex between the Sputnik brotherhood and sisterhood colleagues. Once, I remember I was staying at the Moscow "Molodyozhnaya" hotel and the receptionist handed me the key to my room. When I arrived at my room, I found a Soviet female already staying in the same hotel room. This was an example of sloppiness of the system. Since Sputnik was in the travel business, my only desire while riding down the elevator was to go and ask the Sputnik domestic travel service if they could get a one-way ticket to Siberia for that obnoxious receptionist for such a poor, sloppy job, but I could have been charged with misconduct and been fired.

Another possible and most plausible explanation to the above female and male hotel accommodation mishap could have been intentional. It was the so-called KGB practice of a "honey-trap," or "sex trap," in law enforcement lingo, when the KGB planted their female agent, informant, undercover stool pigeon, "seksot," (Russian for "secret agent") and tried to trap the intended victim by causing illicit sex in order to compromise that subject, recruit or extract needed, vitally important information and then recruit him/her, the victim. The KGB did audio tape and video tape such victims during sex, then compromise and confront the trapped victims. There were different scenarios of "sex traps," including when a mad, outraged husband or KGB agent broke into the bedroom or hotel room when the victim of the sex trap was engaging in sex with the KGB female operative. I am happy to report it never happened with me so it did not work against me. Most likely that was the plan in the case when they tried to accommodate me with the Soviet female in the same hotel room, the KGB had very practical goals: 1.To get me in trouble, any trouble with the law for soliciting sex 2. allegations, accusations, indictments would have been filed against me in that situation 3.the case definitely would have been reported to "Sputnik" management at all levels, including my home office and KGB, and I would have been fired with the "wolf's card," i.e. Russian for being blacklisted for the rest of my life and my career destroyed 4. the case would have been reported to my family members and my marriage would have been also damaged or destroyed 5. I would have had zero chances to defend or prove myself or hire an attorney to defend myself against KGB's allegations and accusations. Russian attorneys defended the Soviet Communist system not the people. Many of my good friends who graduated from law schools in the USSR gave up their law practices and became teachers or college instructors. in order to avoid serving the Soviet injustice system; 6. I still remember well and will never forget that female, would-be hotel roommate, whom KGB planted in the same room with me and had malicious plans for me. She was tall, well-built, strong posture and combat-trained. She was a well-trained army soldier, head up, shoulders straight, military, ready for action, a Russian heavy-weight lifter and ready to kick box. She had sandy colored hair. Surprisingly, when I unlocked the room to enter, she was there standing behind the door, waiting for me. This proves that the scheme and the ruse were all planned in advance to trap me maliciously. Her smile and hospitality easily showed her professional training in legal and illegal entrapments. "Honey-traps" and flirting were just the openers in her rich, diverse arsenal, but I did not become her victim. I did not bite the bait.

Working as full-time in-country host guide-interpreter, I had a huge advantage and great golden opportunities. I was learning the cultures of different countries and learning and improving my language skills, including American English. My job as full-time guide-interpreter working with foreign visitors and delegations from different countries from all over the world, including Western, gave me great opportunities to make friends, stay in touch, correspond with people outside the Soviet Union (although definitely subject to Soviet censorship). I met our American sponsors through my job as an interpreter and tour guide for their group while they were visiting Russia.

I did correspond with my foreign friends who were tourists from the Netherlands and I served as their guide-interpreter. It was a Dutch family who sent my older son, Ilya, and me private invitations in 1989 to visit the Netherlands, though the notorious OVIR did not issue us exit permits and did not allow us to travel outside the USSR. Our plan was, while visiting our friends in the Netherlands, to be looking for a job, for a contract while utilizing my linguistic skills.

Western tourists and visitors, all Western groups, were of special status designated by the KGB and travel agencies while visiting USSR. "Special Attention Status" meant, you, Peter, pal, guide-interpreter, pay special attention to the Westerners and make them happy. At the same time Western visitors were the best evidence and testimony to Soviet citizens that KGB, the Soviet Government and official propaganda could not stop. The testimony and evidence that Westerners were bringing a mental picture to Russia on a daily basis regarding a higher living standard in the United States and other Western countries. The evidence showed proof that their clothes and footwear were of much higher quality not to mention of their freedoms and liberties that they enjoyed. Westerners seemed to be happier, more relaxed and calmer compared to their Russian counterparts, most of whom were sad, gloomy Russians.

Many of those Western visitors became my friends, my guides, my interpreters of various aspects of Western life, history, politics, and economics including helping me improve my English. Yes they were that generous and I was that open-minded. The Westerners became my conduits, my allies, but hold on, stop here BUT (and it needs to be in all capital letters) official Soviet propaganda and KGB tell Soviet people: you cannot be a friend or ally with the USSR's major, most dangerous adversary, the United States of America. No, it was recorded in the Soviet official military doctrine that you cannot do that, you cannot be their ally. If you are, if you become the USA's friend, in your mind, in your mentality, you have betrayed the Soviet Union, you are traitor, you betrayed Lenin, Stalin, Brezhnev, the long, long row of Soviet Communism's bloodiest dictators, tyrants and despots. You are in the danger zone; you are in the Iron Curtain country where they rule with iron fist.

The Soviet Closed Cities

Possibly you know this term, "closed city." Typically, a closed city in the USSR involved defense industry plants, enterprises, military units, companies, stationed troops, KGB border patrol troops, special detachments, special operations troops and multi-purpose military training facilities. These closed cities were run, governed and managed by the Soviet government, its military authorities and agencies. It may be surprising to you, but these cities were closed during the Soviet period not only to foreign tourists, visitors, officials and foreign diplomatic service personnel to avoid exposure and leaking of Soviet secrets, but also closed to their own, Soviet citizens. Soviet closed cities were considered to be of high security risk and secret defense industry enterprises, nuclear plants were located there. Gorky, now Nizhniy Novgorod, was a closed city and it was so convenient to arrest, deport and exile, in January 1980, the world-renowned Soviet academic, Nobel prize winner Andrei Sakharov and his wife. No foreign reporters, no foreign officials were allowed to go to the closed city of Gorky and visit Sakharov.

When I was a tour guide-interpreter, I had many opportunities to visit at least one closed city, Ungheny in Moldavia. It was a small town on the border of Romania and Moldavia and it had a big presence of KGB border patrol troops. It was normal for the Soviet Union to charge KGB troops with the control of Soviet borders. Every time I had to go on a business trip to Ungheny, I had to file an application and submit papers to the local police department for a domestic visa to visit. I had to declare the reason of my trip ("official business"), so I could go and pick up the tour group there that arrived typically by train. In one particular case, KGB troops were looking for different things and they took the border patrol and control seriously: smuggling, contraband, drug trafficking, narcotics, crack, marijuana, dope, various types of weapon smuggling, apprehending international terrorists and criminals, all wanted by different Soviet and international agencies, including Interpol. Soviet customs office clerks also had certain assignments: to prevent and stop counterfeit money from abroad, smuggling of illegal items such as precious stones and ivory.

Soviet-Era Syndromes

1. Stalin Syndrome - to arrest and try to imprison or murder everybody and turn the whole country into a Gulag prison camp.
2. Suspect, suspect everybody without any respect or aspect.
3. Suspect, suspect everybody, everybody, everywhere, everything—they are there, everywhere, in every bus, in every street car, every trolley-bus in every train, they are there to get you, everywhere, because it is the Soviet Union, Soviet Communist system, where your every word, sentence, gesture, eye wink, breath, body language will be recorded, bugged, intercepted, wiretapped and reported to the Soviet Communist authorities, ultimately, to the secret, dictatorial, tyrannical despotic police, the KGB.
4. Do not trust anybody, anywhere, in any situation, under any circumstances. You are in the Soviet Communist Union, you are under the Communist system (see #1), suspect everybody, everywhere. There are spies, stooges, informants, under-covers, saboteurs, provocateurs, provokers, plainclothes, pigeon stools, KGB agents, spies are spying on spies, spies are spying on their bosses, on their subordinates, spies are talking about their own spying business, everybody spies everywhere, dog eats dog, wolf eats wolf, lion eats lion, everywhere, in every office, in every Communist party grass-root organization, in every city, town, village, location, in every company, every station, in every train station, every bus station, airport, at every show and entertainment facility. The Big-Big, Very Big, Brother, Mr. Big, is watching you and over you, everywhere openly and secretly.
5. Self-censorship when writing an article, essay or book.
6. Self-editing
7. Self-preservation
8. Self-restraint when writing

9. Severe, cold war type censorship with full-time, well-paid, government-sponsored, government-run iron curtain. Closed society censorship, Iron Curtain Society. Closed society surveillance.
10. Big Brother is watching over you, your wife, your mother, your neighbor
11. Suppression of all freedoms, liberties, freedom of word, religion, speech, assembly.
12. Alcoholism was mass and typical, 74 million dypsomaniacs during the Soviet-era period—heavy alcohol drinkers, unreported by the Soviet Propaganda. Alcoholism was considered a crime and not treated. No alcohol treatment or rehabs, just jail and imprisonment time.
13. Cold war provocations and initiations

Tenets of the Official Soviet Establishment

1. Ideological warfare.
2. State-government-sponsored falsehood, lies, falsifications, libel, slander, rumor, campaigns, sabotage
3. Planting saboteurs, spies, stooges, undercover, sabotaging
4. Kharakteristika"—(Literal translation: Character profile, summary of the character, personal and professional skills.) The official reference letter in lieu of a personal CV or resume as it is known in this country: the official reference becomes an official file with four major mandatory, required signatures: A. by the boss of the Communist party of the USSR local branch division; B. by the boss of your company general manager C.. by the trade union boss, D. by the AYCL—All Union Young Communist Leninist League
5. Stay away from the personnel department and fear it like hell
6. "To give somebody a Russian look" means to say nothing, not to answer a question when asked.
7. A very popular Soviet-era syndrome, called "Boss-absence syndrome."
8. Do not laugh or smile as you may be disturbing somebody, something, somewhere, your bosses maybe interpreting this as a

plot, as an attempt to sabotage and destroy the Soviet communist regime and be careful, watch for trouble out there.

9. Personal space—your physical space and distance between you the person next to you, either talking to you, standing next to you, serving you, laughing or whatever. Most of the people did not observe it. I was told that the synonyms for "personal space" are "pragmatics" in social linguistics. Possible explanations: most Russians did not own their own cars; they had to use public transportation systems of buses, street cars, or trolley buses which were always overcrowded and packed like a can of sardines. Brawls and fist fights are typical. Russians followed the notorious herd instinct as to follow the crowd and act like the crowd..

10. Do not speak freely, do not talk—just whisper, whisper, it will help, it may help not to be heard by the long, long ears of the KGB and maybe not be reported for whatever reasons. Do not share anything with your neighbors because you cannot trust anybody and they may report you to the authorities for whatever reasons.

11. "Schadefreude," a condition, state of mind, of being happy while another person is miserable or at the expense of someone's tragedy, misery a reflection and synonym of the Soviet reality and mentality. This was another Soviet syndrome.

In Love with the USA

At some point in my life I fell in love with the USA, its language, American English, its heroic, glorious history, its freedoms and liberties, its lifestyle. But it was not a safe love when living in Communist Russia. Here is my love story in a nutshell: it all started in my fifth grade in 1964 when our school administration was assigning fifth grade students to foreign language classes. There were two choices: English and French. By God's choice and luck my class was assigned to study English. If I had been put in the class that was assigned to take French, probably I would have had a different destiny. I fell in love with English from the very beginning. It was love at the very first sight and it is a never-ending, ever-lasting love. I fell in love with the English language and the United States of America so deeply that as early as probably in 1966, I put a tattoo in between my thumb and index finger on the top of my left hand by using my right hand for the writing and some dangerous India black ink. I stayed sick for several days thereafter. My tattoo reads my name "PETE" in English. That, for sure, made me a candidate for being blacklisted with the KGB later in my life.

"No, you cannot do that. You cannot use the adverse language, the hostile language, the language of our adversary. You cannot do that, you cannot do a tattoo in English, even if you were trained to speak English. Forget it, forget your skills, forget your linguistic expertise and experience. This is a dangerous language, a globally dangerous language that our enemy uses daily. You cannot use it, do you understand that? Memorize that, remember that! Because one day we will get you and we will remind you. Mark my words! Just mark them!" This is how the KGB, the Soviet Government and the propaganda machined talked to me and delivered the subliminal message to me and my family. There was a time when I was suspected by the KGG of spying for the United States. The day the KGB and the Soviet Government threatened me did come. It was the day when my family and I got a legitimate contract from the USA Information Agency from the University of Alabama in Birmingham Center for International Programs. The Soviet OVIR authorities, told me: "No, this is a private contract. You cannot go. We cannot allow you go to the USA. You, your body, your brain, your blood are our property and our requisites. You cannot do anything." That is how they communicated with me.

Important People in My Russian Life

Fyodor M. Dostoyevsky

Could you imagine that F. Dostoyevsky was outlawed in the USSR during the Lenin-Stalin-Khrushchev era? He believed that man could be saved only through his faith in God and that's why his heroes are believers in God and adored him. Dostoyevsky was confident that all woes in Russia originated and were deeply rooted in atheism, denial of and nonbelievers in God. Dostoyevsky foresaw the collapse of the Russian empire, deviation from God's worshipping and he forecast the arrival of Communist, atheistic system, headed by the Lenin

Government which could not stand any opposition, especially from the Christians.

I loved Dostoyevsky and had many volumes of his writing when we lived in Odessa. I could not bring my library from my home when we came to the United States and left there many volumes that I bought in different cities in the USSR when traveling around the country. I had his diaries, Brothers Karamazov, Crime and Punishment, Gambler, Idiot, Netochka Nezvanova, White Nights, Deprived and Underprivileged. I remember sending books by Fyodor Dostoyevsky books to my friends in the Netherlands and Bulgaria. Fyodor Dostoyevsky was the most popular Russian classical writer. He was considered the best at describing, exploring and revealing the mysterious Russian soul In the West.

Fyodor Mikhailovich Dostoyevsky's writings were banned in the USSR because of his faith in God and his denunciation of socialist and Communist ideology, including atheism and the entire Communist system. The Communists considered him to be pessimistic and anti-Socialist. I visited the grave of Fyodor Dostoyevsky. It is symbolic that he was buried in the graveyard of the most famous Russian monastery. Thousands of Russians followed his casket to pay their highest respects to the greatest Russian writer and the poet of the mysterious Russian soul, who himself was involved in political clandestine activities with the Petrashevtsy Club against the Russian government. He was sentenced to death and few minutes before the execution the Tsar's envoy delivered the message that Fyodor Dostoyevsky's death penalty was replaced by a life sentence to the Siberia settlement reservation. What a tragic story; what a brutal treatment of the greatest Russian writer of all time.

Dostoyevsky, like other Russian writers Leonid Andreyev and Ivan Bunin, was outlawed in the USSR. Ivan Bunin had applied for a Soviet citizenship after he had been approached by Konstantin Simonov, a great poet and war writer. Bunin, after long hesitation and struggling with his feelings, agreed to return to the USSR after being subjected to Soviet diplomatic manipulations. He died in 1953 in France in bleak poverty begging money to pay for his food and bills. He considered the Bolshevik Revolution of 1917 to be a real insult to the Russian nation. Some writers like Alexander Kuprin and Aleksey Tolstoy came back to Russia. They were among only a few Russians, who had lived in the West, repatriated and were not charged with espionage charges and betrayal of their motherland and who did not undergo the ordeal and atrocities of the Gulag and Soviet concentration camps under Stalin. Aleksey Tolstoy was very popular during the Second World War agitating against German Nazis and inspiring Soviet soldiers and people of all ages and walks of life to defend the motherland and fight desperately the enemy.

Alexander Solzhenitsyn

Solzhenitsyn was also religious and was sharply criticized by Communist authorities. The Y. Andropov KGB agency planned to murder him but Solzhenitsyn was very popular in his country and especially in the West and was granted tremendous support by Western governments, primarily United States politicians and human rights activists. Soviet authorities formally decided to expel the author of "Archipelago Gulag" to the West.

I recall a funny story in conjunction with Solzhenitsyn and other Soviet writers. A Soviet writer caught a golden fish that fulfills wishes in exchange for its freedom. He was an elite, Bohemian, party-establishment writer who owned a luxurious car, a big apartment in a prestigious old town area, a pompous dacha summer residence in Yalta on the Black Sea and had a great amount of savings in several bank accounts in Soviet and Western banks. His only wish from the golden fish was to expel Alexander Solzhenitsyn from Russia. "You are a real fool," said his wife after she heard what her husband asked for from the golden fish. "You'd better asked for talent," she advised him.

Vladimir Vysotsky – Russian Poet and Bard

Vladimir Vysotsky was extremely popular in all sectors of the population and among all ages in the USSR and many other countries of the world, mostly in Eastern Europe during his lifetime, 01/27/1938 - 07/25/1980. He was and is still very popular in many countries, especially the former Soviet Union. Vladimir Vysotsky was the symbol and epitome of integrity, honesty, honor, fairness, justice, optimism, survival and dignity in the kingdom of darkness behind the "Iron Curtain" of the Soviet empire. He was the Soviet bard, also called "The Russian Bob Dylan."

Vladimir Vysotsky challenged the official Soviet establishment by his biting satire, creative work, his honest and sincere songs, lyrics, poetry and the roles that he played in movies, TV serials, drama theater and by his own life. He had to pay a high price for that: obstruction, censure, total control of his life and creative work and mind control. Till the end of his days, the government controlled the roles he played, questioned and censured his lyrics and scripts and would not let him perform his very popular songs (in the style of bards, he was a chansonier) in big concert halls, but just in small, underground rooms. He was a "refusnik" denied the right to travel outside the USSR till he married world-famous French actress of Russian descent, Marina Vlady (Marina Vladimirovna Polyakova). The Soviet suppressive regime did not allow Vladimir Vysotsky to publish or print a single book of his poetry and writings while he was alive. When Vladimir Vysotsky visited New York City, he was interviewed by ABC's then anchor Dan Rather and asked about his criticism of the Soviet official establishment. Vysotsky denied his role in criticizing the Russian regime. He knew very well that his every word would have been reported by Soviet KGB operatives in the United States at that time. He was definitely afraid of the Soviet official establishment, which considered him to be a trouble maker, an enemy at home in his own country and the enemy of the nation.

I had been accredited to serve as the interpreter and translator for the 22nd Summer World Olympic Games in Moscow in July 1980, when Vladimir Vysotsky died on 25 July 1980. It was a shock for many Russians who dearly loved Vysotsky and considered him to be an icon and a bright ray of hope, a bright light in the Soviet kingdom of deep darkness. No Soviet media published Vladimir Vysotsky's obituary except *Evening Moscow/Vechernyaia Moskva* squeezed, and then only one line that he passed away. If you check documentaries and newsreels on the internet, you will see that there was a heavy presence of Soviet police during his funeral. The Soviet regime feared Vladimir Vysotsky even when he was dead. There was an area of the Taganka Theater where Vysotsky's casket was displayed but heavily patrolled by the police. There was a strong, heavy cordon of the police during the visitation and plainclothes and KGB undercover agents were trying to subdue any protests against the Soviet authorities.

Eyewitnesses stated that the Soviet police drove his casket at the speed of more than seventy five miles per hour to the Vagankovskoye cemetery, his burial place. Soviet authorities were afraid of him, of possible protests and riots. Vysotsky was considered an enemy and trouble maker at home, even when in the casket, and the Soviet regime had a unique experience of handling and suppressing different types of "trouble–makers," from early Lenin's bloody executions to dictator Stalin's Great Purges" mass terror.

Bulgarian Dissident Writer Radoy Ralin

How closed, tightly controlled was the Soviet Communist society? Here is an outstanding example: while I lived in the USSR I did my best to read the press, follow the media, to stay abreast of the latest trends in literature, culture, politics, economy, social life, but we, in the Soviet Union had no knowledge of the struggles and battles of the Bulgarian dissident writer, satirist, humorist and playwright Radoy Ralin whose legal name was Dimitar Stoyanov. I did get to know details of his life, struggles and creative work. How? Initially I learned about Radoy Ralin by word of mouth when I worked for the International Youth Travel Service. When I was the in-country host guide interpreter for foreign delegations from various countries, including visitors from Bulgaria, Radoy Ralin was a so-called "banned writer" who was outlawed in Bulgaria due to his sharp, biting satire and criticism found in his epigrams, one-liners, satirical works, plays and his protests against Bulgarian Communist party (BCP) doctrines, propaganda and severe censorship. Ralin was severely harassed, badgered, ostracized, maltreated and banned from publishing anything he wrote. As part of his punishment for criticizing the Bulgarian Communist Party, Ralin was interned and deported from Sofia, a major city, to the remote countryside where he was closely supervised by the police. His mail was censored and his contacts with people were supervised and limited.

I was lucky to read his works and had the privilege to translate a few of his satirical pieces, epigrams and humorous aphorisms. I got them due to my friends, Bulgarian tourists who verbally told me then or showed me his small books. I wrote them down on my own. Through tourist whom I met and who knew a relative of Ralin, I got a book autographed by him in late 1980's, when he was rehabilitated, that is, returned to

Russia. Ralin was instrumental in the years when communism collapsed in Bulgaria. I pride myself on knowing firsthand the works of this great dissident and protest writer during the dark ages of communism in Bulgaria. Ralin did his best to contribute to the fight and struggle for the freedoms and liberties. Radoi Ralin (1923-2004) was a rare voice of dissent in Communist Bulgaria, a Bulgarian true patriot, a poet and satirist. He was born as Dimitar Stoyanov but used a pen-name, Radoy Ralin. He wrote several humorous poems and anecdotes of good vs. evil. One of his most popular books, "Hot Peppers," contained epigrams criticizing the communist regime. Soon after it was published in the mid-1970's, the work was seized from bookstores and destroyed by order of the Communist Party. His witty and biting epigrams satirized the ignorance of the communist rulers and gave Bulgarians trust in the values of freedom, but they also led to a seven-year publishing ban, obstruction and public humiliation against Radoy Ralin.   He was among a group of Bulgarian intellectuals who was hosted by the French President Francois Mitterrand during his 1989 official visit to Bulgaria at a "dissident's breakfast," one of the signs that preceded the collapse of communism.

Inna M. Saburova

Inna Markovna Saburova was the wife and later, widow of General Aleksand Nikolaevich Saburov who was a Hero of the USSR. The General earned the highest Soviet military distinction as commander of the partisan detachment in the woods of Belarussia during WW II. That award was typically given for valor, courage, and heroism displayed during combat on the battlefields and frontlines during wartime. General Saburov was considered top brass, a member of the privileged and elite class, which is why he was granted, with his wife, a luxury apartment in a Stalin-era high-rise apartment building, one of seven famous skyscrapers in Moscow. Two other skyscrapers in Moscow were the Soviet Ministry of Foreign Affairs and the Ministry of Foreign Trade. Inna Markovna Saburova was of Jewish descent and was a member of the Saburov partisan detachment in Belarussia during WWII.

I visited Inna Markovna Saburova's luxury apartment sometime between 1978 and 1982. Inna Saburova was a very positive and charming lady and liked me very much once I told her I was married (at that time) to a Jewish lady. We met and got to know each other in 1978 or 1979, when I was host and guide–interpreter for a Bulgarian group visiting Moscow according to their itinerary. It was probably November, during a cold Moscow winter. One of the tour group members was a lady reporter who had met Inna Saburova when she visited Bulgaria on several occasions. One of the reporter's reasons to visit Bulgaria was that Inna Saburova had written a book about her WW II experience with General Saburov which was translated and published in Bulgaria. Inna Saburova was involved in some other projects in Bulgaria such as writing the script for a movie made out of her book. Inna Saburova had a great time visiting Bulgaria and made some good friends. I did my best to remember to call on General Saburov's widow every time I visited Moscow.

Inna Saburova was a role model for me. She was an accomplished writer and she was friendly to me for several reasons: my Jewish wife Svetlana (at that time), my writings, my highly-valued, Odessa biting sense of humor, my one-liner writings, our mutual friends in Bulgaria, my Bulgarian ethnicity and many other reasons. We became sincere friends. I enjoyed her intellectual potential and her writings. Not every Soviet citizen could boast such a friend as Inna Saburova, but I consider myself to be fortunate and found myself in many unique positions and situations like this one.

I got the impression from our friendly conversations and my many calls to her, that Inna Saburova was critical of the Soviet bureaucracy and the Soviet establishment, but she reserved her comments to our private conversations and kept her feelings just between us two, without involving her Bulgarian friends, collaborators, writers, ghost-writers, depending on the situation. When I came to the United States I lost the connection with many of my friends in the former USSR, including Inna Saburova. How are you doing today, Inna Markovna Saburova? I hope you are still alive. How are you, my far-far away friends? Where are you now? I cannot find any of you on Facebook. Where are you now?

I.Z. Postalovsky – World War II Veteran

I.Z. Postalovsky is Tosh, Maxim and Ilya Kirchikov's grandfather, the father of my former wife, Svetlana Postolovskaya. I.Z.

96

Postalovsky was barely eighteen years old when he was drafted into the Soviet Army, as a military air mail pilot. Later, he went to fast-track Master Sergeant Technical School and was specifically trained as a tank crew member and sharp shooter. During the WWII he served as a Master Sergeant, tank crew member and military interpreter. He was wounded and burned several times. His parents received a "triangle telegram," the official notice of a MIA casualty. In spite of all adversaries, misfortunes and atrocities of the war, he managed to survive and ended WWII in the heart of Nazi Germany ruined Berlin with other victors of the allied powers, namely with the Soviet Army. Unfortunately, after WWII, in 1952 and 1953, according to his memoir, he was falsely accused by the KGB of being recruited during WWII by Nazi Germany's Abwehr, a foreign intelligence service, as their spy. He was fraudulently charged with spying for them while in the USSR. Postalovsky was interrogated for months, brutally tortured and beaten in order to compel him to sign an acknowledgment of the above, which he would not sign. Only sheer luck saved him from being tortured to death by the KGB interrogators. His former WWII buddy, then a CPSU Party official in Kiev, was visiting the town in Ukraine where Postalovsky worked as a middle school teacher. The buddy wanted to say hello to him but could not find Postalovsky anywhere. He started intense inquiries with the police and local authorities. While the friend was searching for Postalovsky, the KGB came up with a ridiculous scenario of instigating and staging a traffic accident in order to justify I.Z. Postalovsky's multiple body injuries and bruises sustained during the KGB atrocious torture.

I.Z. Postalovsky was very well-known in USSR countries and later, when the Soviet republic dissolved, in the independent post-Soviet countries, and now in the Ukraine. He is one of the most successful initiators, pioneers and designers of the Soviet Russian movement for dynamic reading. This training includes fast reading or speed reading techniques, psychology and moral education and upbringing for school students of different levels as well as psychology manuals for instructors and teachers of all school levels. He has written or co-authored more than forty books, manuals, and brochures on the above-referenced subjects. He is Professor Emeritus of St. Petersburg University, Russia, due to his great contributions to the dynamic reading philosophy, theory and practice. Postalovsky has written two books of WWII memoirs: *This Is My War, This Is My Wound - From Stalingrad to Berlin" World War*

II Memoirs by Master Sergeant, Tank Crew Member and Military Interpreter, 1942-1945. Encounters with the Nazis after World War II By I.Z. Postalovsky. The above WWII memoirs have been translated and published in German.

I.Z. Postalovsky was born in 1923, in Yenakievo, Donetsk oblast, Ukraine, USSR. From May 1942 and till the end of the World War II he participated in the battles against Nazi Germany's fascism. He was wounded three times and decorated with various Soviet military decorations and distinctions for his valor and heroism in WWII. After the war, he graduated from the Law School of Odessa University in Ukraine, USSR, and was trained as the attorney, psychologist, linguist, and expert in the German language, history and linguistics. He authored more than forty books on different issues related to reading, mathematics, teaching methods, foreign language instruction, education and upbringing. Several of his books have been translated into several foreign languages and published abroad. He is one of the founders of the new trend in education theory and the practice of dynamic reading. Postalovsky is the head of the Joint Russian-Ukrainian Laboratory of Innovational Educational Technologies of the International Reading Institute.

Dr. Mikhail Dykhan

Mikhail Dmitrievich Dykhan [pronounced Dyh-hahn] is the Patriarch of the Bessarabian Bulgarians. He was a lawyer by training, a well-known historian, scientist, researcher, writer, speaker, memoirist, my dear friend and a college professor at Odessa Institute of National Economy. My family and I were blessed to have known him and be friends for extended time with Dykhan and his wife. They were a very special couple of accomplished professionals, very talented and unique writers, much-sought speakers and college professors. Mike was also a public figure. Initially, I met Mike in Odessa due to my involvement and work in the Odessa Literary Museum, Bulgarian section. Mike was my mentor and teacher; he was like a father figure and helped me with my writings. I called him and Saida on many occasions, especially when I in 1991, and they in 1992, moved to the United States. They both mentored me and Mike wrote an endorsement and introduction to my manuscript of the dictionary of the Bulgarian ethnic dialect of the village of Krinichnoeyh that I recorded somewhere in 1981–1983. We saw each other at functions hosted by the consulate general of the People's Republic of Bulgaria in Odessa and other occasions.

Mike Dykhan wrote many books that deal with the history of the USSR, Ukraine, Bulgaria, Moldavia, Romania, and Soviet-Russian-Bulgarian friendship that have been considered landmarks and masterpieces. His well-known memoir of World War II is called *I Did Not Want to Die At All*. Mike told me the number of the books he had written, it may be about a hundred of them and some of them, per Mike, were used by the United States colleges. He wrote many books related to the history of the celebrated revolutionaries and public and political figures from Bulgaria who settled down in Russia and the USSR. His writings deal with the history, lore, anthropology, ethnography and folk traditions in USSR and Bulgaria, Bulgarian political emigration into the USSR, but. mainly of the Ukraine, the area known as Bessarabia. In 1972, Mike defended his doctoral dissertation and was appointed chief of the New and the Newest History department of Odessa State University. Since 1975, Mike was the head of the department of the Modern Soviet History of Odessa College of National Economy. Mike has written one hundred and twenty scientific studies and twelve monographies (research papers). Mike's other, well-known books are: *Bessarabian Bulgarians in the October/Bolshevik Revolution and the Civil War,* 1971, and he co-authored *October (1917) and Bulgarian Internationalists* 1973.

Mike was awarded the order "Cyril and Methodius," jubilee and commemorative medals "1300 Years of Establishing the Bulgarian State" and "Forty Years of the Socialist Revolution in Bulgaria." Those are the top decorations in Bulgaria and no doubt, they were well-deserved. Other works by Dr. Mike Dykhan include *Blagoevo Two Hundred Years*, about his native village and *Pod Rodnata Striyaha*, translated as At Our Home, Sweet Home.

Mike Dykhan was born on August 25, 1925 in the family of ethnic Bulgarians, like myself, whose ancestors fled Bulgaria from the Ottoman Empire's five-century oppression in the beginning of the 19th century in Blagoevo, Ivanovsky Rayon, Odessa Province/oblast, Ukraine, USSR, the area historically known as Bessarabia. Mike's ancestors were freedom-loving people who sought a better life and found refuge in Bessarabia, which was part of the Russian Empire at that time. Many years later (almost a hundred and ninety years later) Mike and his family also were searching for freedom, this time from Communist oppression in the USSR and found refuge in this blessed country in 1992. Their son, Igor Dykhan, also arrived with them in this country and currently lives here. On top of his widely acclaimed academic accomplishments, Mike was also recognized as a public figure. Mike's parents were collective farmers, members of the kolkhoz. His father was chairman of the kolkhoz and his mother was a simple, ordinary member of the collective farm.

Mike loved his motherland so dearly and was so patriotic, that he had to fake his age in order to be drafted into the Soviet Red Army for WW II operations. Although Mike was only sixteen, he told the army recruiter that he was eighteen and that got him induced into the army for the long, hard job for four lousy war years against Nazi Germany. He wanted desperately to join the army to defend his home country. I am aware of other similar examples of patriotism and determination to join the Soviet Army to fight against fascism in World War II, even misrepresenting their age. Although the memories of Stalin's great purges and mass executions of 1936-1938 were still fresh in the Soviet people's minds, patriotism was triumphant, dominant, powerful and of paramount significance in Russians' mentality for the entire period of the USSR's history.

Mike was decorated with top Soviet distinctions, medals and orders for his participation in WW II—sixteen medals and five orders. In his well-known, poignant memoir of World War II, *I Did Not Want to Die At All*, he tells the cruel truth of WW II history from his perspective as an ordinary Soviet soldier. He was wounded in the mountains of Slovakia in 1943 and his right leg was amputated. His WWII memoir was published by the Military Publishing House in Sofia, Bulgaria, in 1987 and became a bestseller. Mike gives a truthful, first-hand account of WW II events from 1941 through 1944. His military company was involved in Soviet Army operations in the Ukraine, Caucasus, and Slovakia.

Mike was very popular not only among his readers, academia, professionals and other sectors of population, but also among the writers of that specific region where he lived and lectured and did the most of his research: USSR, Ukraine, Moldavia, Bessarabia, and Bulgaria. He was the coordinator and epicenter of all ongoing, continuous activities and processes related to the Bulgarian ethnic community, its trends and activities. He had a great reputation as the elder, wise man and that is why I called him "The Patriarch of the Bessarabian Bulgarians." I may be not the first to associate Mike with this honorary title that he deserves so much and so rightly. Mike earned this prestigious reputation due to his outstanding dedication to the cause of ethnic minority groups, including the Bulgarian ethnic community, and for his numerous studies, research, manuscripts, books and projects related to the exploration and preservation of the history, culture, traditions, celebrations, ethnicity, ethnography, folklore and anthropology of ethnic Bulgarians of the USSR who were considered to be second class citizens and who did not have any representation in the USSR's Supreme Soviet, or in the Ukrainian equivalent of Parliament. In most of the census polls held during the Soviet period, the actual numbers of the ethnic Bulgarians living in the USSR were always demoted, defrauded, tampered, reduced, defaced, falsified and misrepresented. This was done for several purposes, but the main one was not to let ethnic Bulgarians have any representation, any voice in the Soviet corridors of power in the USSR's Parliament Supreme Soviet or in any other constituent Soviet republic, like in our case, in the Ukraine. Dictator Stalin managed to destroy not only human lives, but also most of the secret and Soviet governmental documents proving barbaric executions and crimes. Most of the census polls of the Stalin era 1924-1953 were also destroyed. Stalin, with his nationalization of land, industries, factories, plants, the national economy and forced collectivization of the farmlands, did not want to show the constant decline in the Soviet population for several decades due to his mass purges and great terror. So much for speaking about Stalin and his attitude, policies, and doctrines towards the so-called "national issue and the issue of the ethnic minorities in the USSR and national schools in the USSR." It's true that there were created in the late 1920s and early 1930s so-called "national, i.e. ethnic minority schools, theaters, cultural and educational establishments in several areas and regions with diverse ethnic groups population." That was the case in the South of the Ukraine, e.g. in Odessa and Odessa oblast, where there were several Jewish schools and a Jewish theater where Yiddish was spoken. Political immigrants from Bulgaria were allowed to found their own Bulgarian theater in Odessa and there were several schools in the Bulgarian villages of the Ukraine where instruction was in Bulgarian. I must disappoint you because all this lasted only a few years and everything was shut down, including the Jewish theaters in major cities, due to Dictator Stalin's paranoia. The actors were arrested and most likely either executed or spent the rest of their lives in Gulag prison camps. As for the Bulgarian theater and the schools, they did not last long either and were shut down before WW II. Speaking about the political immigrants and émigrés from Bulgaria after the September 1923 uprising in Bulgaria, Stalin granted them asylum and USSR citizenship. Dictator Stalin had long-range goals while giving them refuge, he wanted the Bulgarian revolutionaries, who joined the VKP (b), All-Russian Communist Party of the Bolsheviks, to support Stalin in his doctrines and policies. Well-known Bulgarian revolutionaries turned out to be loyal to Stalin, e.g., Georgiy Dimitrov, G. Rakovsky and others, but per reports, because of Stalin's paranoia, his agents manipulated their lives, executed G. Rakovsky and contributed to the poisoning of G. Dimitrov. Some of those immigrants were trained and assigned by the Stalin secret machine to serve as KGB operatives in the international arena and worked for Stalin's Comintern, Communist International, as KGB couriers, in the Spanish Civil War as part of guerilla warfare training camps.

Mike counseled many writers and researchers on various subjects and he was a valuable asset to that community. He also coordinated publishing and printing projects and book ideas that were very beneficial to the above-mentioned area. Mike loved Bulgaria, the land of his ancestors, and equally he loved Bessarabia, in particular the southeastern region called Budjak where Odessa oblast is located. Mike visited many Bulgarian villages, both in Ukraine and in Moldavia, and talked to ordinary people, spoke to different groups and made many presentations on the issues so close to many, if not all, citizens of that particular area. He visited my parents' home when they were alive. He wrote that in his autobiographical book that included also his travel notes and a diary of his travel throughout Bessarabian and Bulgarian villages. Mike had a phenomenal memory and a unique knowledge of a wide variety of subjects. We called him a "walking encyclopedia." His knowledge and memory knew no boundaries. Mike loved singing songs, popular, folk, classical songs in Bulgarian, Ukrainian and Russian while sipping a glass of wine, preferably a red wine that reminded him of his native home-made wine. Mike was multilingual and spoke Bulgarian, Russian, Ukrainian and Moldavian/Rumanian.

I remember how excited Mike was when telling me about his unforgettable meeting with the US musician and performer Van Cliburn in Odessa at the world famous opera and ballet house. I do not remember the details, but I think Mike knew somebody in the Odessa Opera and Ballet Theater, maybe an opera singer, ballet dancer, orchestra musician, conductor or manager, or a staff member who helped Mike approach Van Cliburn through the back, staff-only door. Mike was very happy about that encounter.

Mike died in the summer of 2006, and he was buried in Odessa with much attendance of academia, many professionals and well-known people there. I miss you, Mike, very much, your infectious optimism, your sincere smile, your songs, your jokes, your unique, unforgettable stories, your latest news and detailed reports for the country of our origin. I dial Mike's phone number and want to talk to him again—sad enough, nobody answers the phone. Mike will be greatly missed. I admire his courage, bravery, stoicism and warrior's valor.

Stanislaw J. Letz and His Impact On My Life

Stanislaw J. Letz, born Baron Yerzy de Tusch-Letz, Polish humorist and aphorist, was a beacon, a searchlight, a guiding light in my life, like in the lives of many intellectuals in the USSR and the "Iron Curtain" closed society countries. His unique and dramatic, and I would say tragic, life, his literary works, aphorisms, witticisms, one-liners and poems were a real inspiration, aspiration and motivation for me to survive in the Communist limbo and hell. Stan Letz was born of Jewish parents and from the very beginning of World War II, as a Jew in Poland he was thrown into the Nazi concentration camp and went through all the tortures of the Nazi death camp until July 1943, when the death camp was liquidated by mass executions of Jews and other death camp prisoners. Letz managed to escape wearing a Nazi uniform, he succeeded reaching Warsaw and joined the Polish resistance (Underground) movement. After WW II, Stan Letz kept writing and worked as Poland's cultural attaché in the Embassy in Vienna, Austria. He defected to Israel with his wife, son and daughter, but returned to Poland after two years in Israel. The Polish government obstructed him and mistreated him by taking away his rights to publish and print his writings, but gave them back to him in late 1950's, after Stalin's death. Stan Letz became very popular in Poland and in the Soviet socialist satellite community due to his witty, unique anti-Communist writings, witticisms, aphorisms, epigrams, and poems. His biting humor, his disarming satire and his very sharp sense of humor made Stan Letz extremely likable and popular. It was impossible to find Stan Letz's books in the USSR as they were outlawed and banned by the Soviet Government which did not allow Letz's writings to be published or sold in any bookstore; they were not available in any library. Letz was considered to be the enemy of the Communist Government because he was very critical of the Soviet totalitarian and authoritarian regime. His witticisms and one-liners disarmed and neutralized the Communist watchdogs. They could not keep up with Stan Letz. Below, some examples of his one-liners:

1. "I am against using death as a punishment. I am also against using death as a reward."
2. "In a war of ideas it is people who get killed."
3. "Mankind deserves a sacrifice, but not of mankind."
4. "Never lie when the truth is more profitable."
5. "The window to the world can be covered with the newspaper."
6. "When smashing monuments, save the pedestals they always come in handy."
7. "Value your words. Each one may be the last."

These witticisms, one-liners and epigrams were written and could have been written only by this writer, who had faced death, betrayal, lies, mockery, trickery, falsehood, chicanery and hypocrisy many times. They could have been written only by Stanislaw Jerzy Letz.

My Memories of Nikita Khrushchev

"Know thyself." Socrates

I was twelve years old in 1964, when Soviet Premier and Communist Chief Nikita Khrushchev was brutally thrown out of his Kremlin office, or as it was mildly put in the Western press, "removed" or "ousted" from office. His fall from the tall Kremlin office was the result of a barbaric, medieval Kremlin top-level conspiracy by his deadly enemies, headed by Leonid Brezhnev and the Soviet ideology tsar, Mikhail Suslov. Plotting, secret machinations, ruses and overthrows were part of the Russian ruling dynasty, including Soviet-era tsars. I do remember turmoil, rumors, whispers, uncertainty and the atmosphere of fear during the time when Khrushchev disappeared from the political arena. It happened overnight, and by all measures and tests, it was highly unusual and unlikely for Soviet top leadership to step down. Formally, he was forced to write a letter of resignation and claim retirement, but in reality L. Brezhnev walked with M. Suslov into Khrushchev's office to tell him that the Soviet armed forces, KGB, Navy, and Air Force were on the side of Brezhnev and Suslov and that Khrushchev would from then on be an "honorary pensioner," in Russian lingo a "special pensioner" or "Top Level High-Ranking Retiree" due to his USSR, Central federal government service. It was a huge disgrace for Khrushchev, which he tried to retaliate in his memoirs *"Last Testament: Khrushchev Remembers."* The Brezhnev clique hated Khrushchev and as retaliation for his de-Stalinization and denouncing Stalin, Khrushchev's enemies and opponents did not forgive him even when he died. All Soviet top leaders typically were buried in the Kremlin wall or next to it on Red Square, near the Lenin Mausoleum. Khrushchev was not buried there, but at the Novodevchiy Cemetery.

Here are my thoughts:

1. No doubt, Nikita Khrushchev gained initial popularity due to his unforgettable "secret speech," that was not released to the Soviet people at that time, in 1956 at the 20th CPSU Congress and denouncement of the cult of personality of bloodiest dictator Stalin and the so-called "de-Stalinization" of the USSR, but which in reality meant amnesty and forgiveness to the victims of all numerous brutal Stalin's crimes. That meant that Nikita Khrushchev opened the doors to most prison camps to release innocent victims and release documents of false accusations, indictments and charges against many, many millions of innocent Soviet citizens. That gave closure to some or most Soviet citizens who were victims of Stalin's great purges and mass exterminations. My dear friend, Saida K. Mishurieva, Mikhail Dykhan's wife, was one of them, whose family went through all circles of Stalin's hell. Saida's father, after many months of interrogations, tortures, beatings and atrocities by Stalin's NKVD secret police death machine, was murdered and his body was dumped into the river. No documents, no traces were left by the Stalin death machine

2. Nikita Khrushchev had many enemies and opponents, Brezhnev and Suslov being numbers one and two. They could not forgive him the de-Stalinization process, nor his liberal trends. The Stalinists were very much in favor of a strong fist, an iron fist, the Iron Curtain, Stalin's terror of mass extermination and GULAG-style prison camp regime.

3. Nikita Khrushchev gained popularity as a clown, a jester of high government level due to his corn-growing campaign as he promoted growing corn everywhere, even where the farmlands were not suitable, not fertile for such purpose. For that campaign, he was called in Russia "kukuruznoye treplo," Russian for "Corn chatterbox," "corn-growing faker" or "corn faker," "corn-growing fraudster." I do remember pictures of N. Khrushchev visiting Soviet collective farms, kolkhoz and being photographed deep in the fields with his head barely seen out of the corn, to show how high and healthy was the corn, how good the corn crop and how awfully right was Nikita Khrushchev in his corn growing promotion campaign. When he was on an official visit to the USA, he was taken to a farm in Iowa that also grew corn.

4. I was about eight years old in 1960 when the Soviet Air defense shot down the United States U-2 plane. There was much noise. Pictures of the alleged spy equipment used by the plane, the trial in Moscow, the hostility, anger and yelling were staged, promoted and manipulated by the Soviet government run media and propaganda, including Nikita Khrushchev.

5. Soviet media kept mum about Nikita Khrushchev's tapping on the table at the U.N.O. General Assembly session in 1961 when he threatened "We will bury you!"

6. During time off from his government office Nikita Khrushchev was often pictured in his colorful Ukrainian folk style shirt, typically worn by the farmers and folk ensemble performers, singers and dancers. He loved it.

7. Nikita Khrushchev's big size and very overweight body probably today would qualify him by medical doctors as morbidly obese, but at that time, nobody cared about Russian people's health, a healthy lifestyle or nutritious food. It was the Russian legacy. The leaders were not good role models in many respects, including this one.

8. I remember when talking to Soviet army men, both soldiers and officers, retired and on active duty, that they were unhappy with Nikita Khrushchev's doctrine of reduction of Soviet armed forces of all types and services, including Soviet weaponry and stockpiles.

9. Soviet citizens have not heard about Nikita Khrushchev's memoirs, "*Last Testament: Khrushchev Remembers.*" Only by chance I heard about it on BBC or Voice of America due to my knowledge of foreign languages. To my knowledge, the official Kremlin's position was that those memoirs were not authentic. Well, the Soviet government, headed by Brezhnev, wished that *Last Testament: Khrushchev Remembers*" was not authentic, because the memoirs were truthful and they were a very sharp accusation and incrimination against the Soviet communist system. The Soviet nomenklatura, the Communist hierarchy, did not like it; they did not want to admit the self-incrimination part. Soviet media kept mum as usually and especially about Khrushchev's brutal removal. There was a lot of whispering, hush-hushing during Khrushchev's removal and what looked like his disappearance at the beginning. We knew that something went really wrong to have the top Soviet boss stripped off all his posts. He was a very decorated and highly respected national and world public figure. It was brutal and unusual as we tried to figure out on our own. Definitely, we could not find any information in the Soviet media to give a truthful account of what had happened with the plot against Nikita Khrushchev that resulted in deposing him from the Kremlin office. The official government statement that Khrushchev resigned on his own volition due to health problems was laughable, a joke and nobody believed it, because all Soviet leaders were notorious and well-known for their poor health and none of them retired as they all died while in the office. Many years later and only in this country I was able to do the research that helped me unveil the cruel mystery of the plot against Nikita Khrushchev.

We were not familiar with the following statement by Nikita Khrushchev: "*The Communist system must be based on the will of the people, if the people should not want that system, then that people should establish a different system."*

In February 1958 the Nikita Khrushchev government abolished the MTS, Motor Tractor Stations whose tractors, equipment park were used to serve the kolkhozs and sovkhozs (state farms). All the MTS equipment were sold to the kolkhozes. Nikita Khrushchev imposed on the kolkhoz restrictions the amount of the private land available to the kolkhoz and the food, produce, vegetables that they can sell in the market. It forced collective farmers to rely more on the collective income and less on the earning from their private plots. That agricultural reform was not successful and appreciated both by the farmers and the urban residents who were compelled to shop at the farmer's market since the government stores were bare and the government was not able to provide or manage the supply of foods to the people.

Collective Farm, or Kolkhoz in Russian was agricultural artel of independent laborers to sharing the profit and liability. Artel is a cooperative of workers and farmers under the supervision of the government. Collective farms were artels started in 1929 after the Communist Party's 16th Congress that signaled the forced collectivization, spearheaded by the dictator Stalin. In this context it is the agricultural producers, cooperative enterprise. Initially they were industrial cooperatives among itinerant workers, but later were extended to collective farms and artisan artels. A collective farm is a huge cooperative made up fifty percent of the USSR's kolkhozs. To my knowledge, all Soviet collective farms were located in the rural areas, like our village of Krinichnoeyh, Bolgradsky rayon, Odessa oblast, Ukraine, USSR. Theoretically, they were managed and operated locally by the village based collective farm administration, but in reality they were heavily managed and governed by the CPSU Party entities and organizations. Sovkhoz, sovietskoye hoziayistvo, was the collective farm's counterpart. The difference was that sovkhoz workers were on the government's payroll, but also located in the rural areas.

Comrade Death

The top Soviet leaders either died as a result of long lasting ailments and diseases or were thrown out of the office as a result of conspiracy. Lenin first was wounded during the two attempts on his life

108

and later died while still in office; Stalin died mysteriously while in his office; same with Brezhnev. Khrushchev and Malenkov were removed by force from office by the plotters and their rivals; Khrushchev was under house arrest, became a pensioner and *unperson*, as *Time Magazine* stated. It is the correct term for the unique Soviet phenomenon, actually let me make it plural: phenomena. We have a unique event, an unprecedented historic incident when the entire country, the Soviet Federation, the Soviet Communist Empire disappeared in Dec., 1991, and its President and the General Secretary of the CPSU, Mikhail Gorbachev, lost his job. Actually, he was fired and brutally removed from his office as a result of an unprecedented top secret conspiracy carried out by his former four subordinates who hit the last nail into the USSR's coffin: RSFSR Russian Soviet Federative Socialist Republic's President, Boris Yeltsin; Leonid Kuchma, the Ukraine's President; N. Nazarbaev, Kazakhstan's President and V. Shushkevich, and Byelorussia's President. They claim they made real history.

No other country in the world experienced such a long lasting generation of senile, and dysfunctional Soviet leaders as the seventy-four year period of Soviet degenerate leaders. Gerontocracy is the rule, the form of the Soviet government run by the old, very old, senile, brainless, brain dead top leaders. The Soviet Old Guard of the senile Soviet leaders queued up in line for their turn to take the helm, more of a new Russian Red Tsar's Imperial crown of Soviet leadership and to become next Kremlin King. Some of the top Soviet leaders died in eighteen months (Andropov) or in thirteen months (Chernenko) after assuming greedy and long lusting power. The Kremlin wall and the Red Square turned out to be the burial parlor, wailing wall and cemetery. The Soviet Old Guard, the ruling and power elite, turned out to be the USSR's fifth column, undermining and sabotaging, derailing its own country, Matushka-Rus, Mother-Russia, from within. But for the Soviet people, being the victim · of the totalitarian regime, Comrade Death and perpetual mortality of the top Soviet leadership were a vicious circle in Russia, something inevitable and never-ending, everlasting. Russians did not see the light at the end of the long, dark tunnel.

The Soviet National Radio, known in the West as the Moscow Radio, feared to play classical music which was typically associated for Russians with the death of the old Soviet leaders, which happened often. Believe me, I lived there. This uncertainty is well understood if you take into consideration the fact that the health or rather, poor health of Soviet leaders, was a top secret and leaks were not allowed and actually did not occur. The exceptions to that were high psychiatric and physiological, political profiles and analyses of Soviet leaders compiled by the Western experts, Kremlinologists, prosopographic psychologists, hired by the intelligence agencies whose jobs were to monitor the health of Soviet leaders and report same to their Western United States and British counterparts.   Comrade Death (a Soviet pandemic disease) claimed the aging, super-aging, declining health and perpetual mortality of the Soviet leaders. They, like tornadoes, hurricanes, twisters and storms were daily companions of Soviet leaders and turned Soviet leadership transitions into continuous, non-stop, nightmarish leadership crises. For Russians it was like a daily routine, like dumping the trash, brushing your teeth, washing your hands or working out. You get used to it, or as they say in Russia, life makes you get used to it.   You may ask: why are you writing about this depressing experience? It was part of our life, our sad and stressful life.

Russians love classical music and gave many talented composers and musicians to this world: Tchaikovsky, Musorgsky, Rakhmaninov, Shostakovich, Prokofiev, Shalyapin, Richter, Rostropovich, and Oistrach. Many Russians are avid theater goers; they go to the opera, ballet and other shows regularly to hear and enjoy Russian and world classical music. The Soviet National Radio, called Moscow Radio in the West, often played classical music or recordings of Soviet classical performances. But Russians were very often confused when classical music was played as part of the official good-bye, and funeral ceremonies of another top Soviet leader. These occasions had been arranged and mandated on a nationwide scale. You could hear mournful, classical music from loudspeakers everywhere in the country, in major public places, in squares, at train stations, airports, bus stations, and major buildings. The traffic, especially at airports, was paralyzed, many or all flights were canceled for security reasons or to avoid a coup or an attempt to overthrow the headless (because of the death of the current Soviet leader) Soviet government while there were on-going physical and political fights and battles inside Kremlin corridors of power and outside the Red Square for the Soviet helm to be called next top leader.

My first cousin, Vasiliy Mirchev and I, found ourselves stuck in such a dead-end mess at Vnukovo-2 Airport outside Moscow on the day of Soviet leader Leonid Brezhnev's death in November 1982. We were on our way to the Siberian city of Blagoveshchensk to bring the body of Vasiliy Mirchev's son and my nephew, Vitaliy, who was murdered in peace time while in the Soviet Army. The officer who was a disgruntled alcoholic and fired shortly afterward by his Army bosses for mismanaging the military unit where Vitaly had served his second year. The officer murdered my nephew as revenge for his firing and to make it sour to his bosses at that military company that was involved in construction of well-known BAM, Baikal-Amursk Railway It had many thousands miles long, with military, strategic and geopolitical purpose because the railroad is located very close to the Chinese border. China and the USSR had several military conflicts, including shootings and fatalities in the late 1960's on the island Damansky. Actually, the city of Blagoveshchensk is pretty close to the Chinese border, where Vitaly's military unit was located. All the flights at Vnukovo, like at other Soviet airports, were cancelled and Russian passengers were stuck in the airport with no choices of going to a hotel or anywhere to sleep. They were sleeping on their luggage, on the floor, smoking, playing card games and lining up for Soviet tea, a watery milky diluted version of instant coffee at the airport. There were not any hotel accommodations at the military base so when we arrived and the military put both of us, Vasiliy and I, in a small, primitive trailer. As if the murder of our relative, Vitaliy Mirchev, was not enough, the military base where we stayed turned off the heat overnight in our trailer and we spent a miserable night in subfreezing Siberian winter with approximately -30 thirty Celsius, i.e., minus 22 Fahrenheit. That was the Soviet Army experience.

We managed to bring Vitaly's body to Odessa and do his burial. As a warrior, I managed to hold up through his burial. I even went to work next day, but got sick due to the sub-freezing Siberian cold winter and had to ask my boss to let me go home. Per some statistics that I remember, approximately 13,000 Soviet Army men were killed in action in Afghanistan, in the very unpopular Soviet-Afghan war. The same number, 13,000 Soviet Army men, were killed in peacetime, not on battlefields and in combat, but as a result of murders, accidents, suicides, military exercises, other incidents. Such was the life we experienced.

As Ralph W. Emerson was quoted by President Ronald Reagan on Dec. 8, 1987, while welcoming then Soviet Communist Chief and President Mikhail Gorbachev, *"... there is properly no history, only biography."* I agree, and I would add: there is properly no history, only biography and maybe autobiography.

Hagiography was a typical Soviet phenomenon to idealize, idolize and glorify its leaders. No doubt, Soviet leaders were hagiographic, but not charismatic, except maybe Mikhail Gorbachev. Actually hagiography in Russia was hypertrophied and distorted to the megalomania point, called "cult of personality" that crowned the bloodiest dictator of all times and self-proclaimed Generalissimo Stalin. Look at both Lenin and Stalin; they both became Soviet icons, idols, gurus and "vozhds," leaders of the all people, as they called themselves. Which people? Leaders of which people? Not my people, not my family. I would not like to have them as role models.

My Alma Mater, Izmail State Teachers College

September 1st is Knowledge Day in the USSR at all levels of schools. Celebrating Knowledge Day was a tradition and WW II veterans, CPSU Party veterans, writers, celebrities would come to schools and speak.

I chose the English language as my major and my profession, originally as ESL, English as a Second Language high school teacher. My life goal was to eventually become a linguist and to excel in my life and to succeed in this country.

Of our teaching staff members, professors, instructors, teachers, most of them were home-grown and trained on the job by the senior teaching staff from our college with only a few had earned the equivalent of a Master of Arts or Master of Science degree.

Books, manuals, a language lab, the "London Polish course" with audio magnetic tapes, various equipment, adapted and abridged versions of American and British literature works were available to students: *"Sister Carrie"* by Theodore Dreiser, *"David Copperfield"* by Charles Dickens, *"Citadel"* by Archibald Cronin and John Forsyth were among the required readings for our classes in English of the American and British literature and curricula.

112

My early surprise literary award at ISTTC in September, 1970, as soon as I entered the college, was for a written paper that I submitted to the Ukrainian National High School Student Literary Contest which was dedicated to the history and lore of the Ukraine and Odessa region and Bulgarian revolutionaries staying in Odessa.

Some of my college professors were real characters and we had fun. They impacted our classes and eventually, our lives. Among them, Yury Mikhailovich Felichkin (Latin, French), Anfisa Maksimovna Ovchinnikova (English, Conversational English), Valentina Mikhailovna (?) Komogortseva and a Visiting Professor Andrey Alexander Korsakov, a WW II veteran who worked with US counterparts on the USSR's behalf on a Lend-Lease Agreement as the interpreter and translator and used US dialect in his instructions. He was the author of several books of grammar and theoretical Grammar. A full-time professor of Odessa State University, Professor Korsakov impressed our students and the staff immensely; Lidya Pavlovna Polyakova, our English Language instructor, Conversational English, Lexicology and Lexicography. Each class of students was assigned a staff member to supervise students' grades, behavior, college life, compliance with college attendance rules and policies. I do not remember the written policy about attendance rules, exams, tests, re-taking tests, exams, poor performance, or any agreement and contract that students signed with the ISTTC.

Izmail State Teachers' Training College, called Institute v. University, was middle-size, higher education establishment by Soviet standards with a total number of under a thousand students at all schools, called faculty in Russian. There were about forty universities in the USSR across the country that offered four to six-year education in approximately 343 majors. Our college offered a four-year curriculum program. During the Soviet period until 1991, the course of training was ten years, but after the collapse of the USSR, the education system was highly centralized and run, like everything in that country, by the Big Brother Government. The educational system allegedly boasted total access for all its citizens, free tuition and guaranteed employment and job opportunities after graduation. The Soviet education system was dominated by the Marxist-Leninist ideology and controlled and supervised by the CPSU with its damaging dogmas and doctrines.

There were three levels in the Soviet educational system: Elementary schools were called in Russian "beginning" level, "*nachal'noeye obrazovanie*": four and later three classes. 2nd level: secondary with the seventh grade and later eighth grade classes required to complete the school, in Russian, "*nepolnoye srednee obrazovanie*." Education was compulsory for all children in 1958-1963 and optional for the undereducated who could attend evening schools. Since 1981 complete secondary education of 10 classes in some Soviet Baltic republics was compulsory. Some facilities formed so-called secondary specialized education, '*srednee spetsializirovannoe obrazovanie*.' PTU, *professionalno-tehnicheskoye uchilishte* were vocational schools and trained a wide range of skills like mechanics and hairdressers to apprenticeships and as journeymen. Completing PTU after primary school did not provide a full secondary school diploma or route to such a diploma. In November 1958, education reforms were introduced in the USSR adding practical training to the secondary school curricular. The planned increase of the compulsory 7-year secondary education to ten-years has been dropped and an 8-year system was introduced. Post-school training has been increased and the number of correspondence and evening students increased to exceed the full-timers.

"*Korenizatsiya*" is Russian for indigenization, a policy of the Soviet government, Sovnarkom, of the early campaign for literacy and education. On 12/26/1919, V.I. Lenin, as the head of the Sovnarkom, Soviet Government, signed the decree introducing the new Soviet policy of "likbez," the "elimination of illiteracy" in Russia. The "*Korenizatsiya*" policy lasted from the mid-1920s until the late 1930s, encouraging the use of non-Russian languages in the media, government, education and schools. In order to combat Russification, its goal was to assure native-language education as the quickest way to increase the educational level of future generations. In the 1930s, a big network of schools was established, called in Russian "national schools," which stood for "minority-based and ethnic minorities' schools" and that trend continued and the school networks grew, combining the native language and bilingual education. This, however, was not true for the village schools where I grew up and for the most part of Bessarabia. Why? Because Bessarabia was incorporated into the USSR and colonized during the WW II, in August 1944, by the Soviet Red Army. There were no national or ethnic minority schools in our village or in Bolgradsky district or nearby during the Soviet era. Bulgarian, the mother tongue of the 99,99 % of the villagers, was not the language of instruction during

114

the Soviet period of Communist rule. Russian was the official, Big Brother language of the state, the national language, with Ukrainian being the second native language of the USSR's constituent Ukrainian Soviet Socialist Republic. The Bulgarian language did not exist for the official Soviet establishment and any attempts in Bessarabia, Moldavia, Ukraine by the ethnic Bulgarian and other writers, linguists, intellectuals and college professors to bring up this issue with official authorities ended up destroying either their careers, their plans, dreams, goals, activities, creative works or their lives. There were many ethnic minorities except the Bulgarian one in that region where my parents and I lived: ethnic Gagauzes, Albanians, and Moldavians. This official Soviet policy bruised our lives and did affect my professional linguist life.

In the late 1950s, there was a tendency of growing conversion from non-Russian schools to Russian as the main and official Big Brother official language of instruction. Schools of all levels in the USSR were government owned. The Soviet education was free, i.e. no tuition at Soviet schools of all levels, but the education was free at the expense of the taxpayers, which meant all the Soviet citizens had to pay very high taxes for the so-called free education, free medical, health care and public transportation. High payment in taxes meant that Soviet citizens brought home little or nothing on their payday: my parents as collective farmers, members of the kolkhoz, collective farm, monthly would bring home fifty to seventy rubles depending on the period, e.g., 1960s-1970s. Education was not free in the USSR; it just got paid by taxpayers' money, through different accounts and names. Our college was of middle size and did not have even a military training department, equivalent to the ROTC (Reserve Officers Training Center) in the US. When I was drafted into the Soviet Army, I served one year as a private, not as an officer, like graduates of other, bigger colleges and universities where they had the equivalent of ROTC, called a military training department at that time.

September 1st, the Knowledge Day in the USSR at all levels of schools in the USSR –it was the tradition and WW II veterans, CPSU veterans, writers, celebrities, et al. were invited to come to the school and speak. The teachers and school administration tried to make the day memorable and create a festive atmosphere. Students and parents would bring flowers, smiles, and good moods. But deep in our hearts students were not excited about something: the almost three-month summer break, called vacation in Russian, was over and the drudge and grudge were back in business. We were not happy about some of the classes and subjects that we had to take—all of them were mandatory per the Soviet education system. We did not have choices or electives like in this country. There were classes that were hated by every, or almost every, student, classes related to Marxist-Leninist ideology and the history of CPSU and Soviet Communist Party dogmas and doctrines. How can you like these mandatory classes? No reasonable person could like them. Here is the list of such classes' part of my curricula that were mandatory in my college and in most or all Soviet colleges: History of the CPSU, Political economy, dialectical and historical materialism, scientific communism, history of Marxist-Leninist philosophy; atheism, science of education; history of the USSR from the CPSU doctrines.

I was the first in our family to go to college and graduate. My sister was the second to accomplish that—she went to a correspondence, distance learning, extramural college in Odessa. Why did I choose to go to Izmail State Teachers' Training College, which became my alma mater? My parents, especially my father, dreamed all the time that I would go to the medical school, graduate from it and come back to the home village, get married, settle down and start my own family, my own life, which would make my parents very proud of my accomplishments. "Why medical school?" My father answered this question this way: because my parents, like all other collective farmers, had no healthcare facility or treatment locally and remotely and in case of serious health problems, they needed immediate medical attention, supervision and help. Having a son trained as medical doctor would have been of great benefit and a dream come true for my parents. While I liked medical science, my fascination with languages prevailed and at the end of June 1970, I was heading with my high school diploma and transcripts to the foreign language department of my future alma mater, Izmail State Teachers' Training College. Why did I choose the foreign languages school to major in English and minor in French? Living and being raised in the multiethnic community in Odessa region, Ukraine, USSR, where such languages were daily spoken, official, national or mother tongues like: Russian, Ukrainian, Bulgarian, Romanian, while English and French were taught at our high school. Daily we could hear older generation speak Romanian, while Moldavian version of it was daily

116

spoken by the residents not only of neighboring Moldavia, but many adjacent districts and villages. Russian was the Big Brother's language; Bulgarian is my mother tongue; Ukrainian was the official, native language of the Ukraine, one of the fifteen Soviet republics.

We should also remember that the Soviet federation had more than 155 ethnic groups, minorities and nationalities, which gave me a big boost and encouragement to learn and study languages. This Babylon of a wide variety of languages with a huge diversity of the cultures and their unique, sometimes complex and tragic history entertained and fascinated my mind for a long time. I would call that an atmosphere of complete linguistic involvement and emersion. It will be fair also to mention here the role that some of my teachers played at my middle and high schools and even at college. They were actually my role models and helped me form my choice of a future profession, a future lifestyle and served as my role models. I would like to name them: my English teacher at our Krinichnoeyeh middle and high school, Valentina Vasilevna Koleva, who did so much for us and especially for me. She had the courage to do her best to teach the language that was considered to be in the Soviet Union official adversary's territory both by the Soviet Union's official government policy and propaganda and public opinion, brainwashed by the Soviet media. She was the best and I am fortunate that God put me in her class in the fifth grade in 1964, when our school administration made the choice to divide the fifth graders into French or English classes. God looked after me again. She did her best to instill the best knowledge of English and enthused me to love the English language. That was a heck of an accomplishment in the Soviet period, especially in a rural, countryside school, where instruction level and training of the teaching staff were very poor.

It was common knowledge that there was a huge gap in the living standard, including the quality of schooling between the city and rural countryside areas. I remember later, when as full-time guide-interpreter with "Sputnik" I took different delegations on their scheduled tours to factories, plants, daycare centers, colleges, high schools, I will never forget when some of the full-time teachers of English at the Soviet high schools were hiding during such visits. Why? They, the teachers of English, were ashamed to approach the Western visitors, especially native speakers of English, because they might fail communicating and understanding them, although those teachers were trained, at least for four years, to speak and teach English.

Migration from villages to the cities was an eternal problem in the USSR and striking proof that the Soviet federal centralized government management in reality was a mis-management. People living in the villages for years have been trying to escape and run to the cities to find better life, better opportunities, because the villages were dying. This legacy has not disappeared since the USSR's dissolution. On the contrary, it is even more aggravated now. My second teacher was Mikhail Stepanovich Ivanov who taught history and was also my mentor. Outside the class he talked to me like my father, like my life coach, an athletic team coach, as if preparing me for a big life test or national championship. I think he took pride in my successes, achievements and accomplishments at our school. I won several school awards, local, regional and national literary competitions and contests. I loved participating in them. No doubt, there was always a teacher coaching me along with other fellow students or classmates. Mikhail S. Ivanov and my father were good friends and they talked about my future before I made a choice of college and major. Early in middle school my Russian language and literature teacher, Zinaida Petrovna Taranenko, praised my written papers, compositions and even read some excerpts from them to the class, praising me. That was a huge ego booster and enthused me to offer my writings to the local, district, regional and national newspapers. It worked quickly—my pieces were published in the district paper (loosely analogous to a county publication.)

Wait. That was not the end of the story. The newspaper paid me a small writer's fee. I felt like royalty, pun on writer's fee. My first writing experience dates back to 1965 and since then I have been writing almost every day, non-stop. Even more often than not, like other writers, I write at night, I write when I ride if I am not driving (even when driving, I compose, construct a story plot or story ideas in my mind). When I am in a park or mall or when everybody else is celebrating and drinking, I write. Yes, writing requires a lot of sacrifices and writers make that choice conscientiously.

While at middle school I started doing translations, first from Bulgarian into Russian and offering them to the Soviet pioneer (like Boy Scouts) organization newspapers. Later I started translating poetry and humor (Mark Twain, Francis Bacon, J. Leacock) from English into

Russian. There was a small school supply store in our village that had a book section and often I found bilingual dictionaries in English, French, Bulgarian, Moldavian/Romanian and Italian, as well as poetry and literary works of regional and national classical writers, both Russian and foreign. It was the time when I was falling in love with books. There was a chance also to order the books at that store and have them delivered by mail to our house. I saved some money while working in the kolkhoz helping my parents in the summertime which helped me pay for the books and the shipping. The money was given to me by my parents as a gift "for candies and sweets," as my dad put it.

My early experience of loving dictionaries, languages, spending hours reading books in different foreign languages, translating some pieces, freelance writing and being creative taught me a lesson to move forward and dream big. So, when the time came to make a choice where to go to college, it was logical for me to major in English, minor in French and become a professional linguist, lexicographer, interpreter and translator both of technical and literary literature, which actually happened in my real life. The study of foreign languages was the basis of my formative, character-building, crucial years and helped build my character and stamina as a linguist also.

After I completed my lexicographic research, I planned to work on my Master's Degree. I got an invitation in 1983 to be the visiting scholar of the Bulgarian Academy of Sciences' Institute of Bulgarian Language and Literature for thirty days and work in the college libraries and research centers in Bulgaria. Unfortunately, the Soviet authorities had chosen to blacklist me and did not grant me an exit permit to pursue my lexicographic research in Bulgaria, what used to be at that time the most loyal Soviet subservient country. No visa formalities were required at that time to travel from the USSR to Bulgaria. Moreover, the Soviet authorities did not permit any anthropologic or lexicographic delegations or projects to come from Bulgaria for the purposes of researching and recording history, cultural, ethnic relations, folklore customs, traditions, lifestyle in our local Bulgarian community.

I attended and graduated from Izmail State Teachers' Training College, in Russian called Izmail State Pedagogical Institute, from 1970-1974. It was in an old building located on Suvorov Avenue. The city of Izmail was known for its port, maritime fleet, and shipping company and served as the port of call for many boats, ships both from the USSR, the Soviet socialist camp satellite countries and other countries: Austria, FRG, Federal Republic of Germany, Middle East, and Yugoslavia. My recollections of the college I attended are related to a small kiosk, in Russian called a "buffet" located in the lobby of the main building. I do not have a distinct, vivid memory of our college cafeteria or lunchroom. I think it was small room, always overcrowded, with long lines, long waiting – no surprise there. The major memory is that the food was not delicious – no surprise there either. I do not recall any publication on daily, weekly, monthly or any other type of publication published by our college or any department of our school. It was symptomatic of the Soviet culture, mentality and lifestyle with suppression and the non-existence of liberties and freedoms in the Soviet society—i.e. suppression of freedoms of speech, assembly, religion, faith and denomination.

Attendance Rules

I do not remember a written policy or any agreement and contract that ISTTC students had to sign, but we were required by our college polices to attend all classes and take all required tests and exams, and quizzes. If some students disobeyed the college policies and missed classes without valid reasons, a doctor's excuse and logical explanation, they were expelled from the college, which was very rare. If a student failed tests or exams, he had another chance to study and prepare to pass. If that student failed again and did not show improvements, that student was expelled from the college, which to my memory, rarely happened maybe once or twice to my memory. The class professors had their class roster, called a journal in Russian, where they logged in student attendance, grades and academic success. The top grade was "5," "excellent," next to it was "4" or "good," "3" was satisfactory, "2" was bad and "1" was " very bad or unacceptable." I did well at the college and most of my grades were "5s" and "4s," excellent and good, although I had to sweat a lot, especially during my first freshman year coming from a rural school versus city school where some graduates attended so-called specialized schools where many or most subjects were taught in English. Such students had a huge advantage once they entered the college and plenty of time to party, go to the movies, visit buddies and even get married. Most of the students did well at our college. We did not have a system of "study buddy" to prepare for exams together with our college mates, nor did we have peer tutoring or any tutoring available at our college.

But what we did have is what I call "last minute chill-thrill impromptu peer review." We were in the small classroom shaking and waiting for our turn to take the test. Typically, at least one or two of our classmates were with us waiting to take exams. A student would have a long list of all exam questions as our college within the Soviet educational system allowed us to have the list of approximate questions in order to prepare for the tests. The student, typically a girl, would read the question and we all as a crowd tried to answer the question, thus boosting our confidence for the test. No doubt, tons of lecture notes, homework assignments papers and written papers were handy in that waiting classroom. If you came to see that classroom on the test day, it would have reminded you of a real battlefield with some heads chopped, i.e. failed exams and tests. Most of the procrastinators did cramming and staying up all night till wee hours and last minute studying for the tests, then coming in the morning with foggy heads to take the test. Some of the procrastination was caused by heavy drinking, poor organizational skills, and poor self-discipline. I considered myself to be a hard worker and studied hard for all tests and exams, always on my own and it worked.

When I was a third year, junior college student, probably in 1973, I played the lead role of the English language professor Henry Higgins in "*My Fair Lady*" by George Bernard Shaw. It looks like my college professors sensed my deep love for the English language, which is why they chose me for that role. Our cast did well as everybody was in high spirits. The audience, our English language instructors, professors, administration, staff members, the lead instructor who was also the producer of the show and ultimately we, the students and performers were pleased. You could imagine such plays and shows were not typical at our alma mater, except for special occasions and celebrations: New Year, 8th of March, Women's International Day, and graduation (no prom parties). I will not forget the show and my stage partner, Eliza Doolittle, a doll, cheesecake, candy, very attractive Southern belle, who spoke very good English, and me going to the flower market, shopping and finding a great bouquet of red roses for her, per the play script. The show was over, the faculty, the audience, students and the packed house congratulated us for a job well done.

Later that night, after the show, when I was happily tired and heading back to my dorm room, my female stage partner bumped into me in the hallway. She was in her negligee, smoking and carrying tenderly my red roses close to her right, barely covered breast. She approached me face to face, breath to breath and said she was looking for me all this time. Her face and cheeks were red blushing, not because of her makeup and performance, but because of a good dose of booze. She gave me very intimate hug, a sort of a cootchy, hootchy-kootchy, kissed me on the left cheek, stamping it with red lipstick, and made very a dubious offer, wanting to thank me for being such a great stage partner and especially for the lovely roses and for the English lessons. She said she had a celebration dinner for both of us in her dorm room and her roommate was out of town for the weekend (the latter part was probably a special arrangement). Clearly, she was drunk and I could smell her alcohol. It is sad--drowned roses, lost lessons, lost in translation, lost generation, intoxicated flowers. Sorry, I do not take volunteer drunk sacrifices.

Where are you now, my dear, My Fair Lady? You said, your fiancé was posted in a South African country and you are waiting on him. Did you get married or did the long distance kill your engagement and love? Did you have kids and are they ok? Did you get rid of your drinking problem or did you become an addict like the other seventy four million unreported Russian dipsomaniacs and heavy drinkers in Russia? Do you know that your native place, Moldova, is now is a foreign country to our alma mater, Izmail, Ukraine? Who could imagine that in 1973? Do you still speak English and which language is now your mother tongue and which one is your native or near native language. Is it Hebrew, Yiddish, Russian, English, Moldavian, Romanian, Ukrainian, Greek or Polish? What is your home country now and what is your adoptive motherland and what do you consider the country of your origin? What are you doing now? I hope, you are ok, have a family, children and grandchildren. Do you go back to our alma mater? If so, say hello to our professors and instructors on my behalf. I miss you all. They did a very good job teaching and training us under those circumstances. We were like fraternity and sorority. Sad story. George Bernard Shaw did not script that scene and I'm not sure he would have approved it. I could not anticipate that his character would act like that in real life. I may want to write my own script-sequel to *"My Fair Lady."* Just kidding.

Since my last acting experience I fell in love with teaching English lessons. Since then I taught thousands of English lessons to thousands of students from all over the world, I brought millions of flowers to my wife, mainly relatives, friends, co-workers and other important persons who played a significant role in my life. But, My Fair, Fair Lady, the Southern Belle, is still with me, in my mind. She still keeps me company daily and keeps me busy. She is with me in my car, in my office, while walking and exercising, she keeps me up all night, she still wants to celebrate with me our success, she enthuses me to run across the town and buy her fresh cut roses. She does not like Internet communications, as she wants to see me in person and to smell the real roses from my real hands, not from the computer or TV screen. Where are you now, my dear, My Fair Lady?

My college professor had chosen me for the major role of Professor Henry Higgins in *My Fair Lady*, although I was not best male student at our school, although I did well and was very diligent and stayed busy and studied hard all my home work and lessons. My college professor had a great vision by instilling in me love to English. I not only majored in English, but the English language played the major role in life and became my life career and made me a better person.

College Life

My college years at ISTTC were the best and most formative years for me and prepared me the best way for real life. I learned a lot and not only about my future trade, but also something that my life and status in the village did not and could not provide. My memories of our student dorm are unforgettable. It was an old, L-shaped, one story building with an outhouse in the middle of the dorm court yard which was a landmark. By the standards in this country that building would not qualify for a dorm and would not pass any building code requirements, hazard or environmental inspection. The design of the dorm building reminded me more of an old elementary school in Russia than a college dorm that I have seen in other Soviet cities and was very unusual.

The dorm rooms were packed with five to seven and even more students in the same room, as it was in my case. The girls' rooms accommodated five to six students in the same room. No suite rooms or apartments were available in the dorm. The dorm rooms did not have air-conditioning and the outhouse toilet was right outside our dorm room about sixteen meters and we could smell the odor. My memories of our dorm are of it being noisy, overcrowded and over packed. We had a so-called Lenzal, i.e. Lenin Hall, a home study room named after Lenin (they named everything after Lenin in Communist Russia). The home study room was the only place you could do homework assignments and it was always noisy there. The black and white TV set was always on till wee morning hours, the girls were gossiping and being inconsiderate without paying any attention to anybody either studying or trying to help each other or preparing for a test. Heavy drinking was one of many problems in the USSR and also seriously affected Soviet students. Our dorm was no exception. We had several roommates who had serious drinking problems and failed their tests and exams. They were talented, gifted students and did well at school, but because of heavy drinking problems and hangovers they missed classes and got in trouble because of the violation of the college attendance policy. They would come back home to the dorm room late at night, disturb our homework or sleep. They would bring strangers, some of them of dubious character, when everybody was sleeping. It got very weird and inappropriate. None of roommates reported the violator, because it was considered not safe. I do not think any student in our dorm reported such cases and the management was aware of the situation unless there was a threat of a possible or immediate crime or problem, they did not care much.

One other thing that you might find very strange was our dorm was run by our college administration and the chief of the dorm, called the commandant, was a World War II female veteran. She tried to impose a military discipline in the dorm which did not work. In most cases the chaos resulted in raising her voice and yelling at students to scare them which did not work either, but caused her to swallow more and more whatever pills she was prescribed. The college students residing at our dorm were, per the dorm management and college regulations, were obligated and had the duty to serve as non-paid security guards at the main entrance of our ISTTC dorm. We were assigned a shift per day. Your college year determined how often and how many hours and shifts you got. The guard duties included not letting any visitor into the dorm premises and making sure visitors waited in the small waiting room while you go get that student to come to meet that visitor. If the visitor was the student's relative, then the visitor had the right to visit with the dorm student but the student could not bring the visitor into the dorm room. Somehow, now and then we would see visitors, clearly not of our dorm residents and much older than college-age students. I do not remember crimes committed on the dorm premises. Some crime did happen in a new dorm was during my year at the college, but I did not live there. Other violations included instances when some students sometimes would bring in some girls who were of dubious behavior.

There was no campus at our college but there was a library and books were available through a book loaning system. It was a small library in a small building that had two wings, one for the library and the other was flats for our college instructors. The college repository consisted of mandatory reading books for all divisions of our college and departments—English, French, psychology, child psychology, philosophy, and the Marxism-Communism doctrines. Most of the required reading and mandatory books for our English division curricula were published in English in the USSR, either abridged or in full text, same as the original works. Most of those English-language books were by the classical writers: George B. Shaw, Jack London, William Shakespeare, William Thackeray, and Charles Dickens. The numbers of copies were limited and there was always a waiting line and a waiting list for books to check out. I do not remember any monetary penalties for overdue books at our college library.

Lessons Learned from My Mother and Her Legacy

Lesson One: Do not expect manna to fall from the sky into your mouth. You will have to get up, get out of the bed, go make your own living and bring food home to feed your own family.

Lesson two: Our house is not a restaurant and I am not your servant. You will have to get up, go to the vegetable garden, pick up the items and make your own meal. Do not expect your mother or father to do that as they have their own hard work to do.

Lesson Three: My mother would often say: "Blood does not thin." The Russian word for word translation: "The blood does not turn into water."

Meaning: value your roots, your origin, know your roots, yourself, value your family, immediate and extended, value and respect and honor your parents, grandparents, elders, neighbors. Respect older people, because one day you too will be an old person and how you treat the old people, will count towards the legacy that you will leave behind you for your children and the coming generations. We mean a lot to each other as relatives. These are your blood relatives, your roots, treat them the way you want to be treated—apply the Golden Rule. I was told the opposite to the saying: "Blood does not thin" would be "Blood is thinner than water…" Sad.

Lesson Four: My mother would say: "Even the snake would wait, let you finish eating your meal and then bite you…" Meaning: be patient, be considerate, be reasonable, be logical, do not rush people, do not rush to judgment, do not hurry, do not jump into quick conclusions, when you could use your common sense, your good will, good intentions, instead of rushing and judging people.

Lesson Five: My mother would say: "Take care of your house, clean it, repair it, do not let it get rusted, dirty, run-down. Otherwise, one night when you are going to bed, you will see the moon in your bedroom. How come? Because of the disrepair you will have a big-big hole in the ceiling of your house, right in your bedroom." Very wise lesson. In Russian the word for word translation: "Gol kak sokol…" which means, i.e., the person, who does not care about the house or himself/herself and the household.

Lesson Six: "Early to bed, early to rise, makes you healthy, wealthy and wise." Do not sleep late. Get up and get out of the bed, go and do your work, do your job, take care of your business. Meaning: do not stay up late, do not play or waste your time with computer and video games, TV, Internet, digital gadgets. Read more books, use your brain 100%.

Lesson Seven: "You do not belong to the royalty, you belong here, to our family, to your parents' family." We are not well-to-do, but we are doing our best to take care of our family and our needs. We care about you and you should honor us. Have some respect for us, your parents, who are taking care of you and doing their very best to raise you, to send you to school, to give you high school and college education. You need to go and get your own job and have to work hard to make money, to feed your family, to establish yourself in the society, to earn a good, honest reputation and offer trustworthy services.

Lesson Eight: My mother used to say: "The sun is partying in your bedroom, it is 10:30 a.m., wake up, even the royalty are up. What are you waiting for? It is time to get out and work hard and not to lie in bed or drink your beer."

Lesson Nine: My mother used to say: "If you cannot say a nice, positive, motivational thing about a person, your friend, your neighbor, a family member, do not say anything at all…" I rendered this to my dear American friend and she commented: "Peter, we Americans also say that: If you cannot say anything nice about a person, do not say anything at all. So, it is nothing new to us Americans." "Hold on," I said to my dear friend. "The reason that I am using my mother's wisdom, sayings, proverbs, life philosophy and witticisms in my book is very valid. My mother, like my father, was my best role model in my life. Formally, my mother, like my father was not educated, she was actually illiterate, she never went to school; like my father, she never went to the library, never read a book, never was read a book. My father had a chance to go to two or three night classes, but that did not get him anywhere for he could not read the letters of the Russian alphabet. My parents were forced by the Stalin dictatorial machine to join the collective farm and work there for the rest of their lives, digging in the dirt, using their hands as the only tools of the trade. My mother never spoke English, was not familiar with American or English sayings and proverbs; nobody educated her in US or other world folklore. My mother never visited the US, so she would not be familiar with US sayings. But for me and my siblings, my mother was the most educated and the wisest person in the whole world. No wonder my book is dedicated to the blessed memory of my two dearest people in my life—my highly treasured mother and father.

Lesson Ten: My mother used to say: "I told you so…" her word-for-word saying: "I know/knew that; I just do not know when I will die." By saying so, my mother meant to advise us to be careful, cautious, attentive, caring, considerate, loving to each other and to our parents, others, to help out each other, to be a strong family. Dedication and bondage meant a lot to my mom. My mother would use this saying as a warning against any possible trouble. I would agree that my mother knew almost everything, she knew much and true, she did not know how and when she would die. Unfortunately, a tragic accident took my mother's life on a cold, snowy winter night in January, 2003.

Lesson Eleven: "Remember, if you want to lose your friends, relatives, lend them money. The lesson is simple: do not lend them money or you will lose both your money and your relatives, friends.

Lesson Twelve: "Remember, the greed has big eyes. Do not let greed control you. You should be in control of your feelings."

Lesson Thirteen: "Remember, other people's money is always more expensive." Translation: people are more hesitant to lend you money, less likely, to offer you financial help. Be on your own, be a big boy and take care of yourself and your own needs, including financial problems.

Leaving Home

Departure & Arrival – The Real Price of Freedom

"If God be for us, who can be against us?" Romans 8:31 KJV

It was a warm, shining, superb day when my family and I arrived in Atlanta, Georgia, on September 22, 1991, the greatest day in my life. We arrived after our departure from Moscow by way of Frankfurt-on-Main, Germany. It had been a freezing and a nasty fall week when my family and I left Moscow in sharp contrast to the sunny Southland of America. My two sons, Ilya, age fourteen years old and Tosh, a twenty-month-old, and my now ex-wife Sveta and I had all been extremely cold in Moscow. We stayed initially in the hotel Molodyozhnaya in North Moscow. A group of Russians saddened our departure as they were drinking heavily and partying the whole night. The men were very noisy, screaming, and yelling. They used the same suite bathroom we did. One man fell asleep on the toilet seat and spent the rest of the night sleeping there, thinking it the coziest place in the world.

The suite was stinking and I asked the dezhurnaya (the floor clerk on duty) to help us. She promised to do so but in reality nothing changed. The next morning the hotel receptionist demanded that we vacate the room where we had been staying for three days. I tried to reason with her as we were waiting for our US entrance visas and did not have a place to go with two children. The management did not want to listen to our arguments and kicked us out of the hotel.

128

I had spent many nights and days in this hotel when I worked for the Sputnik International Travel Bureau for almost fourteen years until January 1991. Hotel Molodyozhnya was built in the spring of 1980 specifically for the 22nd World Summer Olympic Games, at which I served as an accredited guide-interpreter. The hotel was considered one of the best, along with Orlyonok, another Sputnik hotel located in Southwestern part of Moscow. That hotel housed the USSR's Sputnik Bureau's national headquarters, near Vorobyovskyie/Lenin Hills. Hotel Molodyozhnaya was located on Dmitrovskoye Shosse (there are no interstates in the USSR). Both Molodyozhnaya and Orlyonok were designed to accommodate visitors and delegations mainly from Western countries. In fact, I had been on a business trip at Moscow's international airport, Sheremetyevo-1 sixteen months before our departure from the USSR and had seen long lines of smiling and laughing foreign tourists, business people and Soviet officials, all well-dressed, serious and self-confident VIPs checking in for international flights.

The August 1991 coup lasted three days and by September we saw long lines there again, but the atmosphere was gloomy and so sad that the building itself seemed to be not so well-lit and the travelers not so luxuriously clad. They did not smile; they were far too serious to smile or laugh. There were ethnic Jews, Georgians, Armenians and Germans of different ages, all with pieces of luggage, and waiting many days, frequently checking their names to be sure they were on the list for two weekly Aeroflot flights to New York. They clutched their letters from INS, the US Immigration and Naturalization Service, for which they had waited many months, or years, to be placed in the annual quota of Soviet Jews to move to America. In a matter several hours, they would become Soviet émigrés (those who were leaving the USSR for political reasons) and American immigrants.

Meanwhile, people in America were speaking of forthcoming hunger in the USSR, possible pogroms (mass persecution and massacre of certain ethnic minority groups, mainly Jews, both by the czarist imperial Russia and the Soviet Union. The notorious society "Pamyat" (a word which means "memory" - but very short memory) calls itself historical and patriotic but is in reality chauvinistic, anti-Semitic and nationalistic. It has strict rules: the eligibility "fee" to the organization is to provide home addresses and phone numbers of two Jewish families in the USSR. Pamyat was allowed to hold its rally on Red Square in

Moscow two years earlier (in 1989), something which had never before been allowed. The society published a newspaper which was not registered under Soviet law. It appeared the Soviet Government, its protégés and patrons were comfortable with the Pamyat status and acquiesced to its notorious actions and activities.

In my job I traveled 150 to 170 days annually, a big part of the year torn away from my family, and always had to deal with low performance and poor service quality in hotels, restaurants, trains and tourist buses. My kids badly wanted me at home for my time, my attention, my quality time to play with them, to hug them, to go to movies, museums, theaters, and circus shows. It was stolen time for my children were robbed of part of their childhood. Even though I had experience staying in the government hotels, my family and I had to find other accommodations until we were able to leave the country. Sveta had relatives who lived in the suburb of Moscow who said it would be O.K. to stay at their apartment. I had to carry our big suitcases using overcrowded public buses and the subway. My hands were torn and I was worn out.

While my family waited at the relatives' home, I went to the US Embassy in Moscow to apply for our US entrance visas. There was a long line of Soviet people and some foreigners applying for visas with the militia men (the Russian term for police) in front of them. Soviet police were controlling the lines which had the look of a scared, angry crowd on the verge of besieging the US Embassy in their desperation to get out of the country. About a month earlier, just after the coup d'état, I had called my relative in Moscow before leaving Odessa and asked him about the procedure for visa application. He called the embassy and they told him we should go there, sign in on the waiting list that the Soviet police kept. To see a United States Embassy employee and apply for entrance papers took at least thirty days. I asked my relative to go and put our names on the waiting list because his office was nearby.

"Peter," he said, "the army troops and tanks are in front of my office next to Red Square. I am scared to go to the US Embassy."

I did not blame him. It was August 19, 1991. Nerves were frayed and tempers were hot. The Soviet people were terrified because of the KGB-instigated putsch, that the coup masters would turn the country back to the dark ages and dictatorship, that there would be total suspension of constitutional and human rights. I went to my boss at the

Yugsel Foreign Trade Company (my last place of employment in Russia) to tell him about my legal contract in the US and our plans to apply for Soviet exit visas.

"Peter, where are you going? What are you doing? Martial law is imposed in Moscow. The Soviet authorities will not let you out of the country."

"Never mind," I told him "I will go to Sofia, Bulgaria, and apply for entrance visas at the US Embassy there."

My family and I were very determined to get out of that Communist hell called USSR. Nothing could stop me in those days. Initially, Soviet authorities, KGB foremost, did not allow my family and me to leave the country; nor would they allow me to sign a legal contract with either a Soviet or foreign company to work abroad as a translator. I have training, skills, experience, and the educational background in foreign languages and speak Russian, English, German, Bulgarian and Ukrainian. I can read and understand French, Rumanian, Polish, Italian, Latin and Dutch. My now-ex-wife is of Jewish origin. Being Jewish she was eligible to emigrate to Israel and she could take the family with her. She had a first cousin who had immigrated to Israel, from the Soviet Union, two years prior to when we were trying to leave. We were desperate and needed to get out. Our lives were being threatened. I was a free-lance writer and at that time, the Soviet government controlled all the media and media outlets, including writers in the country. I had been blacklisted because I was married to a Jewish lady, and I had attempted to publish some of my writings outside of Russia, because I had a tattoo with my name in English, (a definite no-no in the view of Soviet authorities), which made me a candidate to be blacklisted, and because I had corresponded with people in other countries (as a youngster I had written to a British student asking to be a pen-pal and that one, innocent act was the beginning of my dossier-building by the Soviet government). The country was falling apart and our futures looked extremely dire. Sveta's cousin went to the Foreign Ministry of Israel on our behalf. They issued us Israeli entrance visas and he sent them to us in February 1991. The visas were seized, however, by the KGB and held till late August that year. It looks like the KGB could not believe that the KGB-orchestrated August 19, 1991 coup failed and they waited for more confirmation of the failure before they released our visas.

In late April 1991, our American sponsors informed us that my contact with UAB, the University of Alabama in Birmingham and visa formalities for our entire family had been approved and we could start the Soviet exit visa procedure and finally my family and I would get a chance to get out of the Soviet Union. Ms. Kay Savage, Paul (Buddy) Burson, Glenda Burson and Edward Robbins sponsored our coming to the United States of America. Initially I got a contract as a visiting Professor at the Center for International Programs at the University of Alabama at Birmingham. At the end of April 1991, contract papers were signed by the Assistant Director of UAB Center for International Programs, Carol Argo. When I took the papers to my boss he said, "Go to the Odessa Regional Authorities' Exit Visa Committee, which was a division of the Odessa Executive Committee located on the second floor of the Communist Party Regional Headquarters. Unofficially, that office was completely run, supervised and staffed by undercover KGB officers. One of them was speaking Italian on the phone when I entered his luxurious office. His boss was very arrogant and had an answer prepared for me way before I arrived at his office.

"No, your contract is a private matter, you cannot go and take your contract in the USA," he said.

"Please, pick up the United Nations Organization Charter that was signed by the USSR as a co-founder and charter member and read what is says about cultural exchange, international exchange, student exchanges, visiting professors and international co-operation," I said,

I went to a law firm and met with an Odessa lawyer. "It is legal," he said. "You should not be prevented from going with your family to take this contract in the USA."

I quoted the Odessa lawyer's response to the Visa Committee bosses, but they were accustomed to rule-control-dictate. They were not inclined to listen to any arguments. Rather, their function was to suppress ordinary Soviet people, to suppress human rights and to separate families. The Soviet dictatorial regime was true to its tenets, legacy and doctrines: they seized and kept our family's Israeli entrance visas locked up till late August 1991, waiting for the real outcome of the failed August 19 Soviet coup.

Those visas authorized us to leave the USSR and move to Israel and eventually to seek adjustment of our permanent residence status to Israeli citizenship. At that time, there was an official organization, the

KGB Letter Reading Unit, of the Soviet government which read all mail to Russian citizens from individuals and companies in Western countries. That office had read my contract papers with UAB, had decided to sign off on the contract but in the process delayed it by several months. After some months of uncertainty and pressure imposed by our sponsors, in the end, they agreed that I could go to the US but my wife and children could not, a typical ruling that served to separate the family. The Russian government was contradictory, fraudulent, hypocritical, and deceitful. They incriminated themselves by changing their stories but the hardship fell on us.

Later I checked with the same exit visa committee. They said: "Only you will be allowed to go to the USA, not the rest of your family."

That answer was not acceptable and we decided to keep fighting. My family could not survive in the USSR at that time of turmoil without me as the main bread-winner. Sveta had our 18-month old toddler, Tosh. My sponsors in America were ready to fly to Kiev, Ukraine, or Greece to meet us and deliver airline tickets for our entire family to bring us to the US. They were afraid of the August 1991 coup and that the KGB and Soviet Communists might kill us before they could get us out of the country. We know now our sponsors' fears were well-founded. Our American sponsors were very courageous, persevering, enduring, and unwavering in their determination to get me and my family out from behind the "Iron Curtain" country and to bring us to this beloved country. During tough times in the USSR, it seemed that hope and faith were fading away and another dark period of Communist dictatorship was landing upon my family (the failed coup d'état of the Gorbachev Government on August 19, 1991). I will never forget when I got a phone call from one of the sponsors who said:

"Peter, I am ready to fly to Kiev and deliver plane tickets for your family, so you can come to this country and start your employment."

It was a lesson for my family in courage, perseverance, determination and never, never, never giving up. Our sponsors gave me and my family a ray of hope; they gave us a bright light in the kingdom of darkness called the USSR. All the sponsors and their families worked very hard to make it possible to rescue us from the tyranny of the Soviet totalitarian and dictatorial regime. The sponsors made it possible for my family and me to make my own American dream come true and live in this great country as new Americans. My grandparents did get a chance to come and live in the USA. Two generations later my grandfather's grandson and his family were fortunate to come to this blessed country with his sponsors' help and pursue their American Dream. Yes, The American dream is alive and well and today I am truly blessed to call America our home, sweet home.

While on their visit to the USSR, one of our family sponsors, Kay Savage, gave me a color, wallet-size picture of herself with US President George W. Bush and the First Lady Barbara Bush. The picture had been taken in the President's office, well known all over the world as a US landmark. The picture had been taken during an executive photo session.

That picture was a guarantee that the KGB and the Soviet repressive machine would not kill me or any of my family members because our sponsors personally knew the US president. The KGB would not have harmed us, because too much was at stake. The USSR, with its political and economic instability and ethnic tension, depended too much on the West, primarily, the US. President George Bush was very popular in the USSR and recognized as a world leader.

In 1991, President M. Gorbachev was overly popular in the West, Gorbomania was everywhere, but not well-liked in the USSR and faced huge resistance by the old guard and because he tried to repair the communist system, to offer cosmetic surgery and preserve communism. The country was boiling and screaming about the state of affairs in Russia. Reforms were not working; communists were clinging to their power, there was big opposition to glasnost and perestroika. Gorbachev had met with then-president Reagan and knew his country could not compete with the West. Gorbachev did not realize that communism did not work for the Soviet people. It was working against the Soviet nation. The Soviet Empire, the monster "evil empire," as it was called by President Reagan, was collapsing, but the KGB still controlled everything and considered people to be their property.

The government wanted to own the people, to control their thinking and lifestyle. They supervised and surveyed in every way. I had been working for the Sputnik International Youth Travel Bureau, which was completely controlled by the KGB. They considered everything to be secret and I was told that even typewriters were supposed to be registered with the KGB. I was suspect because of my profession, because I owned a typewriter, and because I interacted with visitors from Western countries. At times, the KGB seemed to imply that I might be a spy for the West.

I had been writing free-lance since 1960's. I wrote feature stories, humorous pieces, one-liners, aphorisms, research papers, biographies, poetry, verses, literary, technical and medical translations. Everywhere I went I was controlled either by a full-time censor or senior editor, who, being afraid to lose his position, would not publish anything that would jeopardize his or her career. Anything that hinted of discord or in any way, confronted the uncontested Communist Party line was refused. Self-censorship, a strong feeling of fear of being punished or fired for writing something anti-Soviet or against the Soviet official establishment, reigned supreme. The need to be extremely cautious was an everyday phenomenon of Soviet intellectual life. Many Soviet intellectuals were unpublished, ostracized, outlawed, imprisoned, arrested, tried and expelled or deported to the West. Their books were seized. Many Russian writers and intellectuals had to emigrate, or defect, because of the Soviet system of suppressive censorship and total control of thoughts and actions. It was a privacy-free society. Many Russians, including professional translators, experienced difficulties translating the word "privacy" because privacy was not known. Privacy did not exist in the USSR, was not permitted at all. Privacy was not honored; privacy was a foreigner, a stranger in the USSR, the unwanted and invisible alien.

The lack of privacy seemed to be an intruder in the Soviet lifestyle, a disturbance in the daily routine. The desire for privacy was viewed to be a bad habit and official authorities encouraged suppressing privacy. Lack of privacy went hand in hand with intrusion of one's personal and human rights. I often stayed in hotels because of the nature of my job. Many times hotel management unlocked room doors on some pretext or other, without my permission and without knocking. It happened during the daytime and at night. At no time was my privacy respected, honored or observed. Sometimes I was put in a room with a woman I did not know. I don't know if these women paid extra or bribed the receptionist to have a man in their room for money, sex, partying, alcohol, fun or speaking foreign languages. I could provide only knowledge of foreign languages. I was not willing to provide anything else, even if I were tortured. Most likely, it was an attempt to set me up in the "honey-trap," secret police lingo for sex trap, when a female KGB undercover operative acts like a hooker, lures the victim into the room and then during sex the unforeseen happens: a crazy jealous, zealous husband/lover breaks into the room and the classic "Othello" scenario may develop. Being caught in such a "honey-trap" could have cost me my professional career, my marriage, my family, and even caused destruction of my entire life. This type of scenario was not the only attempt to lure me into a trap. I am glad they did not succeed and God looked after me every time I was subjected to similar traps and tricks. The arsenal of dirty tricks and traps was inexhaustible. The imagination of the KGB was very creative and worked for the benefit of their malice. Somehow the KGB always knew the exact time of my arrival at certain destinations, locations, airports, train stations, bus terminals (e.g., Moscow, Leningrad), even the exact hour. They had a list of my personal friends, our relatives, our immediate and extended family members, intellectuals, writers, editors, humorists, satirists, translators, interpreters, performers, and entertainers. Every time I showed up or visited the homes or offices of people on the list, there was always somebody strange, and suspicious, typically a man of athletic posture, a body builder type, either pretending to read a newspaper, book, or magazine or stomping around in circles near the place of my visit and sometimes invisibly and inaudibly talking to his/her walkie-talkie, which was not available to the general public, only to the secret police enforcement.

When exploring opportunities to move to a Western country, I contemplated one more option but did not share it with any of my family members because it was not safe. That option was the possibility of my defecting to a Western or other foreign country that would grant me political asylum. It was a dangerous choice, because in case I defected and was granted asylum, my family members, both immediate and extended, would have been harassed, obstructed and probably hurt or even killed by the KGB. Something would have happened that one could have read about in conjunction with Nathan Shcharansy's family story, that of Ida Nudel (*Hand in Darkness*) or similar to the most recent big story of the Chinese blind activist-dissident, a self-trained lawyer who managed to escape from his guards and seek asylum in the US Embassy in Beijing.

If I had defected and the host country of my attempted defection deported me back to the USSR, it is certain I would have been tried in

136

there by the notorious Soviet justice system and charged "with treason to the motherland" and at the least I would have been sentenced to a long prison term in harsh weather conditions in a Siberian Gulag prison camp where most likely KGB would have planted a fake, violent, gangster-type cell mate who would have killed me in a way the KGB had in their huge arsenal to make it look very natural.

I did not share my plans or thoughts even with Sveta, my wife at that time. I did not share this plan with my sister, my mother, my father or anybody. The reason was simple: if they did not agree or did not approve my plan of defection to a Western country, which would have been the case, my plan would have become known and disclosed to a wider circle of people and KGB had extremely long ears and lots of eavesdropping, wiretapping, listening "bugs" planted everywhere because I had worked at Sputnik International Youth Travel Bureau and because I was considered suspect. You can guess what would have happened to me if my plan to defect had been disclosed to the KGB: I could have been fired, charged with a criminal offense, with an attempt to deceive and defraud the Soviet system by going abroad on a duty trip as an assigned interpreter of the Soviet tourist group and attempting to defect while away. "Treason" was the most popular article of the Soviet criminal justice and penal code and was typically used in situations like this.

I realized it was an unsafe plan and I was very cautious about my thoughts and did not discuss it with anybody. Because my former wife, Sveta, was Jewish and anti-Semitism was ravaging in Russia for more than two hundred years, my defecting to a Western country would have definitely resulted in grave, serious repercussions to Sveta, our children, relatives on Sveta's side (all Jewish family members on her side) and myself. If I had defected, my immediate bosses in Odessa, the Director of the Sputnik IYT Bureau, his Deputy, my immediate boss, chief of the guides and interpreters translators department would have been fired. There was a possibility that some immediate bosses in Moscow Central (HQs) Office IYTB "Sputnik" would have lost their jobs or suffered demotion as well, reprimand for missing the signs, for letting me out of the USSR, for my having the Jewish wife, for my belonging to one of the Soviet ethnic minorities (Bulgarian), my not passing their C.A.R.L. test - Courtesy, Career, Associates, Reputation, Loyalty, which definitely includes patriotism and loyalty to the Russian Motherland and many other reasons that do not make sense to a reasonable person, but were normal Soviet daily practice, unwritten law or secret directive unknown to most Russians.

> *"Eternity may be a long time, but it is nothing compared with communism."*
>
> Peter Kirchikov

"Russian Dream" vs. "American Dream"

By now we know the "Russian Dream." The dream of many Russians to find a legal way to get out of the country, explore a better life and fine better opportunities somewhere outside Russia, preferably in a Western country and hopefully in United States. Russians were ready start all over in a new country, do their best, become valuable citizens of their adoptive homeland and get established there. Recently when I was teaching a class based on my memoir, I was asked question that comes up constantly: "Since life in Russia was so hard, why do not they, Russians, try to move out of the country?"

The answer: in the country that did not sign, until the late 1980's under Gorbachev, the Universal Human Rights Declaration that endorses free travel and free choice of the country of residence, it was very hard, next to impossible, for ordinary Russians to obtain all legal documents necessary to exit the country. To leave Russia requires finding legal, reliable sponsor(s), a legal contract for employment in the new country, securing all Soviet exit permits and going through the unbreakable, omnipotent, Iron Curtain, Iron Rod, Ironclad, Iron Fist, Stalinist-type mentality bureaucracy. The other part of the problem was to secure entrance visas from the host country, health insurance arrangements, job security and immigration authority authorization to enter the host country. Formalities get much more complicated when you have immediate family members joining you to work abroad. During the Soviet period, for common Russians, it was almost impossible to do all the above formalities and exit the country successfully unless a miracle worker was available. Many foreign countries nowadays have adopted so-called isolationist and protectionist immigration laws restricting the influx of foreign citizens and reducing their quotas significantly.

Leaving Home

It was a nasty and cold day and most of my family members got a cold when we left forever our mother country from Moscow International Airport Sheremetyevo.

It was a gorgeous, summer-type sunshine day that God provided for us when we arrived at Atlanta's International Airport on September 22, 1991, welcoming us to this great country that has become our new, dear and sweet home. Our sponsors: Kay Savage, Glenda Burson, Edward Robbins and Paul "Buddy" Burson were waiting for us, happy and smiling, in the waiting area and I could feel their never-ending, staunch patience that had lasted forever, not just fifteen months. It took that long for Soviet authorities finally to release me and my family from the deadly grips and grasps of what used to be called the Soviet motherland.

This was it! Our long wait and long ordeals of many years in Russia were over and now we were receiving a joyful welcoming embrace and delightful hugs from our dear sponsors who are real heroes to us. After our arrival, hugs and happy tears, our sponsors took us in nice luxury van and cars to the house of Kay Savage's family in a well-known area of Birmingham. As I mentioned, it was a warm, gorgeous, cloudless September day. Coming from the Ukraine where the landscape and terrain are characterized mainly by steppes, i.e. vast, treeless, level tracts of black and sometimes red soil and arid, excessively dry lands with serophilous vegetation, the land with no mountains in our region, rivers, hills and evergreens, it was like a paradise to see the evergreens, the gorgeous, green trees, bushes, shrubs of biblical origin, hills, mountains, lakes, rivers, a huge variety of animals and squirrels and chipmunks in the yard. God blessed America with all her wonders!

It was a temporary arrangement for us to stay at Kay's house since the house that we were going to rent was still being renovated–we were just waiting on the final touches. Our minds were so blown away by the modern amenities and many conveniences in Kay's house that we thought we jumped at least a hundred years ahead when we arrived in U.S. We were coming from Russia where my parents and even now my sister's house still does not have running cold and hot water. Kay's house was a luxury and like a paradise island. Our sponsors made us feel very welcome, happy and at home from the very first day of our arrival and did their very best to help us to adjust to the culture of this blessed country. Over the course of time our sponsors have done so much for us and on our behalf that we will always be grateful to them. We will never really know how much they sacrificed for us. We will never be able to repay our debt of gratitude to our sponsors during our lifetime.

Even now, after twenty one plus years in this blessed and great country, I am still amazed and excited at how many opportunities, freedoms, liberties, fortunes and chances to excel and succeed this country offers. One remarkable experience was buying our first home and the sense of owning it, the comfort and the joy of paying it off.

Establishing my credit and consumer history, and getting my first credit card were unique for me. After all, coming from Communist Russia which has no credit cards and no credit consumer history programs, it was all new and a huge challenge to me. Even now, after almost twenty one plus years in the blessed and great country, I am still amazed and excited about the huge opportunities of free enterprise, the way to do business, the protocol and etiquette of doing business, the multitude of laws supporting and creating a healthy atmosphere for doing business, the opportunities to do business overseas, the tolerance and freedom of religion and faith and the multitude of religious denominations and the tolerance of other denominations. What a great country!

For me this country, even now, after twenty-one-plus years in this blessed and great country, is still a paradise, "a shining city on the hill," a beacon of the freedom and the invincible leader of the world, the best place to raise the children and to do business.

Adjusting to Life in America

In Pursuit of Freedom – The Story of Peter Kirchikov

KNOW Paralegal Magazine, May 2009

QUOTE: "One day, my boss said, 'There is a KGB agent who came from Moscow to meet you and has questions.' I was so scared."

QUOTE: "It was the matter of life and death. We wanted a better future and better life for our children and ourselves."

My name is Peter Kirchikov. I am a paralegal and live in Birmingham, Alabama. I came to America on September 22, 1991, from the Soviet Union. I was born and lived in the South of the former Soviet Union, a multi-ethnic federation that is now the Ukraine. I was educated in several languages: English, Russian, Ukrainian, Bulgarian, Latin, and German, and worked as an interpreter servicing delegations from all over the world. I have been freelance writing since the 1960s. In the old Soviet Union, where I was married and raising children, there is no freedom. At that time, the country was falling apart and there were very few resources. We lived on the second floor of a high-rise building but water was only available at certain times. After 7:00 in the morning you will not get water. If you wanted to take a shower, you will not be able to. In America, you take a shower, go to work and the professionals always wear neckties and nice clothes.

I pursued a dream of being a lexicographer, a person who compiles dictionaries but my story is not typical. The atrocities of the Communist totalitarian regime significantly damaged my life as a professional linguist, lexicographer and semanticist. After I completed my lexicographic research, I planned to work on my Master's Degree. I got an invitation in 1983, to be the visiting scholar of the Bulgarian Academy of Sciences' Institute of Bulgarian Language and Literature for thirty days and work in the college libraries and research centers in Bulgaria. Unfortunately, the Soviet authorities have chosen to blacklist me and did not grant me an exit permit to pursue my lexicographic research in Bulgaria, which used to be at that time, the most loyal Soviet subservient country. No visa formalities were required at that time to travel from the USSR to Bulgaria. The Soviet authorities did not permit any anthropologic or lexicographic delegations or projects to come from Bulgaria for the purposes of researching and recording history, cultural, ethnic relations, folklore customs, traditions or lifestyle in our local Bulgarian community.

I began to get many threats on my life. One day, my boss said, "There is a KGB agent who came from Moscow to meet you and has questions." I was scared but I am law-abiding. I will talk to him. She set up an appointment. I came to the office. The agent didn't show up. I breathed a big sigh of relief, at least for that moment.

The hardest thing that happened to me was in April, 1989, when I lost my son, Max, who was only 4 years and 5 months old. He died of sarcoma and leukemia due to the worst nuclear explosion in the world at the Chernobyl nuclear plant near Kiev in Ukraine. A huge number of people died and continue dying in Ukraine due to that disaster.

They believed my son was misdiagnosed. It was Saturday night when he choked and could not breathe. I called the ambulance. It took forever. They took him to the Children's Hospital and diagnosed him with double pneumonia. The next Monday, I was scheduled to travel. I called my boss and said we had an emergency. My son choked last night. I would like someone to replace me. She was not compassionate. I left early Monday. I arrived and a few hours later and they sent a cable that my son had passed away. We did take Max to the pediatrician for check-ups but Russian doctors were not qualified to diagnose anything.

My family and I were threatened, intimidated and harassed by the Soviet authorities for a long time. We have been blacklisted for many reasons, some of them being our ethnic origins and my writing; my lexicographic research work and dream to pursue my career in linguistics; my contacts with many foreigners in different countries of the world, including Western countries during the cold war and many other reasons. My family did not want to live in the totalitarian, dictatorial, narcissistic, despotic, autocratic, tyrannical, oppressive country, the Big House, the USSR. It was the matter of life and death. We wanted a better future and better life for our children and ourselves.

After many years of harassment, intimidation and threats on our lives in the USSR, my family and I managed to leave with the help of our sponsors in the US. We arrived in this blessed country in September,

1991. I got a contract with the University of Alabama in Birmingham Alabama in 1991 as the Fellow at the Center for International Programs.

I remember the events leading up to September 22, 1991, very well. One of our sponsors, Kay Savage, was ready to fly to Kiev and deliver tickets to bring our family to America. We were so desperate. It had taken fifteen months before the Soviet authorities issued the exit permits to our family.

We stayed in chilly Moscow several nights waiting for our flight to the USA. It was cold, misty, foggy. My family members got so cold. The Russian landscape is doom and gloom. Then, we found ourselves in sun-shining, gorgeous Atlanta, Georgia, with probably 80 or 90 degrees. It was like paradise! Our sponsors were smiling and happy greeting us at the airport. I did not think about the formalities like showing the documents I had in my hands. I was carrying our 20 month toddler, (our youngest son), and carrying the luggage. The sunshine, smiles and happiness of that arrival day are still with me every minute.

While I do consider myself flexible, it took a lot to adjust. In the USA, there are many social clubs and charities. I have no memory of a charity in Russia. When you come from a communist country there's no customer service. When you walk into the Russian department stores, no one helps you. It was a striking difference. Everybody in customer service here is polite and there is a sales presentation to sell the product.

When I came to this country, I needed to adjust to the mentality. Fears were part of the adjustment. I thought, "There are so many laws. Will I be able to abide by them?" The first book I bought was the pocket-size law dictionary published by Barron's. I have it to this day, although I get kidded because it has duct tape all around it to keep it together.

Our sponsors bought a house in a very nice area that we rented. Our friends took us to the grocery to shop. My, gosh! My mind was blown away. That grocery store was a huge compound. In 1991, you had bare shelves in Russia. In the states, there was a huge store, multifunctional: a pharmacy! Produce, canned food, fruits, meats, Western Union to send money and other things. And, everyone was very attentive.

Guess what? Most of those fruits were not available in Russia. Oranges and other citrus fruits were not available except in a few shops. Apples and grapes were available only during summer months and you were lucky to get them in October. I thought, "This grocery store could feed all of Odessa!" You can imagine my surprise when I found out that this was not even the only store in the city as there was another one just a few blocks away. I couldn't believe it.

Then my friends took me to the pharmacy. Moscow is one of the huge cities in the world, with 8 million people. I would look to buy small bottles of vitamin C for my children when I was there. I would walk and go to many pharmacies with bare shelves. But when I walked into the pharmacy in many of the American groceries, I thought, my gosh! So many different medications over-the-counter and it's all regulated.

My ex-wife could not adjust to our new life in America and she left in March, 1992. I had to make another adjustment because I had to be on my own with a 20-month-old toddler and a 14-year-old child. Fortunately, my sponsors helped us.

Another big adjustment was the freedom of religion. The Russians declared freedom of religion but it did not exist. When we came to this country, there were so many churches! So many religions! In Odessa, a city of million, there were only four. One was one synagogue. We were not allowed to disclose the location of the synagogue. There was one Catholic Church downtown and one small Russian Orthodox Church. The government always had that cathedral under reconstruction which is how they controlled it. If you were religious, there were people watching you. Our friends here took us to a mega-church with a huge compound, gym, school and library. I was amazed at the gorgeous buildings.

When I was in the USSR, I was so book-hungry! Here in Birmingham, there are many book sales. People buy grocery bags full of books. You can buy a dictionary for example. I bought one for $1.00. It's *The Readers Digest Great Encyclopedic Dictionary.* This is the book of life! You have Spanish, English, pronunciation, and medical dictionary which was all in one book. One of the adjustments was to find a professional job that would be a career for the rest of my life and help me excel, make me happy and allow me to work toward my goals. I had a career counselor, job searching and job hunting counselor. We decided that going to paralegal school would help me realize my dreams and excel in my life. I went to the National Center for Paralegal Studies with thirty-five American students. My writing skills and linguistic skills helped me do well at school and as a paralegal.

.   My advice to other paralegals? Explore opportunities. Know what your goals are. Become an expert. In the future, life will change. People will have to become very proficient, high performing, and skillful to perform their duties. Work towards what you want. Investigate the field. There are many people who can help you. Go meet people, talk to them. Go attend different social clubs and associations like our paralegal association, attend meetings, read books and websites.

My family and I are so grateful to the US, to our sponsors who brought us to this country, to all our American friends, associates and employers who embraced us, stretched out their hands in the hardest time of our lives, took us into their arms and made us feel at home; for the opportunity to live in the world's most developed and advanced country with a high living standard; the world leader.

We enjoy every day, every minute of all the freedoms, liberties and justice that we have here; to wake up and have peace of mind and to know that the rule of law is your protection under due process of law; to be associated with highly professional people; and to see your dreams come true.

This feature story was published in the KNOW Paralegal Magazine, May 2009—reprinted with the permission of the KNOW Paralegal Publisher.

Adjustment to American Culture and System

It was not just defeating jetlag when arriving from overseas, more of a culture shock, more like jumping from a plane without a parachute into the ocean, like jumping from the antiquated Russia of the 19th century, taking a 200 hundred year leap into the technologically advanced USA.

Driving a car in the USA—my big adjustment and the big challenge, struggle and victories.

Writing "Thank you" notes, a long-lasting American tradition, was a very new habit, although being a writer, it did not present a problem for me.

Laughs, healthy laughs, smiles, jokes and kidding that Americans use in their daily lives, in office and business environments, on stages, in theaters, TV, shows, are very admirable and still impresses me.

I love books and the Soviet Union being a tightly closed society and me being a writer and full-time paralegal, I find the US to be truly a blessed country. There is easy-to-find, abundant information on needed subjects with well-managed publishing and printing industries. I find needed books easily here at very affordable prices.

It took us years to get adjusted to the American culture and to succeed and be valuable US citizens. We had lived in the country with a communist, totalitarian regime, with the living standard equal or lower than in third-world countries, with obsolete tools, equipment and technology. Every time my family and I went to eat meals at one of our favorite and family-oriented national franchise restaurants, I noticed and told my wife Carla, about one of the most precious artifacts on display on the walls and on the dinner tables was the oil lamps with wicks and white glass, called kerosene lamps in Russia. We used those kerosene lamps all the time up until the mid-1960's when electricity came to our Bulgarian community in the Ukraine, USSR. The oil lamps were the light to my future because as a boy and teenager they provide me with the necessary light so I could do my homework in my house.

I had studied the history, culture, politics, literature and the language of the USA and other Western, English-speaking countries, e.g. Great Britain, Canada and Australia, as part of my college curriculum and syllabi. Though I actually had first-hand experience working with US and other Western delegations, citizens and tourists while I lived in the USSR I still felt a huge void and vacuum in my knowledge of actual and current culture and reality, day-to-day life in the US. "Why so? How possible?" You may ask. Here is the explanation: we lived in the communist country of the closed society, Iron Curtain with total control of all aspects of life, politics, mass media, minds, and brainwashing including lack and denial of freedom information. We did not have a chance to tune to and watch Western TV stations or listen to their radio stations, read Western newspapers or magazines. We could not go and buy freely the *New York Times*, *U.S. World & News Report,* Only "*Beriozka,*" created and designed for Western visiting citizens, was available in Western hard currency stores in the USSR. Those stores carried a few copies of a few Western newspapers that were not seriously critical of the USSR's regime, current politics and current Communist government. Most of those Western publications were purchased by Western visitors. Routinely, Berizoka stores would carry English-

146

language Communist newspapers printed by the Communist parties of foreign countries, e.g., GBCP, Great Britain's Communist Party's paper, "Morning Star" and the US Communist Party's paper, "Daily Worker." Those newspapers, like their Communist Parties, were heavily funded and supported by the Soviet Communist Party and the Government which was made up hundred percent of Communists. What a surprise!

Sense of Humor

Speaking of adjustment to the American culture, when we arrived on September 22, 1991, I met many people and made many presentations at schools, churches, professional and business clubs. Many people could not pronounce my last name and it was easier for them the name of the current Russian leader, so they called me "Gorbachev," I guess I was that popular. Seriously, Gorbachev was very popular, more in the West, than in his home country and Americans loved Gorbie. So, it was easy for them to pronounce his, Gorbachev's name, than mine. Calling me Gorbachev was nothing compared to calling me "Kryuchkov," the former KGB boss who was imprisoned because of his crucial part in the failed coup against Gorbie on 19 August, 1991. You cannot have it both ways. I am not, I have not been related to any of the above Russian politicians in any way by blood, birth, party or any other affiliation or relationship.

Hammer and Tickle

"In Communist Russia we all were equal: equally poor, equally paid, equally mistreated and equally deprived."

"A Communist is a person who has nothing and willing to share it with everybody."

By all means it was unsafe to joke in USSR, to tell jokes, to write, to recite, to render and to disseminate jokes. Soviet people, especially writers, humorists, satirists, stand-up comedians, actors, intellectuals and performers paid a very dear price. Sometimes with their lives for telling Soviet political jokes. Many were imprisoned in Gulag prison camps and executed, depending on the type and contents of the joke. I had personal friends and knew professionals, full-time reporters, news desk editors and chiefs of the reporters who were obstructed, censored and threatened to lose their jobs, their lives, fired, banned to be published due to their witty, biting and satirical one-liners, epigrams, jokes, and humor books. Some of them like Mikhail Zoshchenko and Mikhail Bulgakov, very talented writers, playwrights, humorists and satirists, were rejected by the official Soviet establishment and government and were banned by the Stalin dictatorial machine from being published in the USSR and were either doomed to die from starvation and depression or were expelled and deported to Western countries because they were considered to be a threat to the Soviet communist regime and its CPSU.

But how did we manage to tell political jokes and survive? We told the jokes in private, in a small circle of family members and loyal friends. We did not share jokes in public, in a big crowd, in the office environment, in college class or at games, in public buses and other public transportation. We practiced PC, political correctness, and we knew the boundaries, the topics, the audiences, the dangers to our lives, and we did not cross the line. Some Soviet syndromes and defense mechanisms kicked in: distrust and suspecting everybody, self preservation and self-censorship. Still, it was not safe to speak out publicly and there were no guarantees that leaks would not occur. It was not safe. The KGB's long ears and big eyes were hearing and watching everywhere and everybody.

Definitely, we used caution and preventive measures, but there was not a guarantee. As a linguist who speaks, reads, understands and writes in several foreign languages, as a free-lance writer writing in different genres, including humor, satire and one-liners critical of the Soviet society, and as a full-time translator and interpreter, lexicographer, I, like other Soviet writers, used self-censorship, self-editing and self-preservation techniques to survive in the Communist society. This was not fool-proof either: I was blacklisted for many years by Soviet authorities. One of many reasons for my being blacklisted was that I wrote humor and satire pieces for a long time starting in the 1960s. Another reason: I compiled, edited, translated and managed to publish fragments of my "Anthology of Modern Soviet Humorous Aphorisms, One-Liners and Witticisms" which included the wittiest and most representative epigrams, jokes and one-liners of famous living Soviet

148

humorists and satirists whom I met, knew, corresponded with or was referred to by other Soviet writers. That was not safe at all, because telling political jokes in the USSR, mocking and making fun of the Soviet Communist regime and its values was considered a crime, a capital offense punishable and qualified "as Anti-Soviet Propaganda" by the Article 58 of the Soviet Penal Code, which basically said, "Pal, you will not succeed by defecting to the Western free world; we will catch you for writing your anti-Soviet political jokes."

Jokes in Russian are called anecdotes—no wonder: they are from real life and down to earth, the salt of the earth. Here is a joke that depicts the Soviet unfair, broken injustice justice system:

A judge runs out of his office bursting into laughter.

A colleague of his stops him and asks what is the matter.

"I just heard the funniest joke in the world…."

"Tell me!" says the other judge.

"I can't. I just sentenced the guy to ten years imprisonment for telling it!"

Forget about freedom of speech and always remember as your boss will let you say anything, if only that pleases his Majesty, the Grand Dictator of all times. Otherwise the rest is qualified as anti-Soviet propaganda.

Ben Lewis's book of humor "*Hammer and Tickle*" put it this way: "*Communism was a humor-producing machine. Its economic theories and system of repression created inherently funny situations. There were jokes under fascism, and the Nazis too, but those systems did not create an absurd, laugh-a-minute reality like communism.*"

Soviet censorship was the king & the queen slashing and slaughtering any type of humor or satire.

Comparisons of Lifestyles in the USA and USSR

The US Postal service and its many competitors offer a variety of services. Certified, registered, hand delivery, courier and the many varieties of packages, envelopes,   the ways official correspondence is arranged and handled; the ways company correspondence is done; the array of official business and business correspondence products and services; document & special handling instructions. There are different designations for different types of mail in this country: personal confidential, private, file, copy, certified, registered and many others. The choices are overwhelming.

In Russia you would be glad if your mail was delivered and no damaged or destroyed. One thing you knew for sure: it was screened, pe lustrated (read by the KGB by its Letter Reading Unit).

Things I am Grateful For

- Being a Christian that can openly worship God
- I am grateful to this Country for letting my family and myself to come and make it our home.
- For great freedoms and liberties that we have in this country
- I am grateful to my parents who gave me life
- To my siblings
- For my family, my wife, my children and the grandchild
- To our sponsors who brought us to this country and gave us a chance for better life and better future
- To our friends, associates, partners and entities who are our life lines, our life coaches, mentors, brothers, sisters, colleagues

Peter's Writings

Welcome: To Life.

Generalissimo Stalin:

I am writing this letter, because I cannot keep silence any more. I want to share my knowledge and experience with those who did not live in communist hell and were lucky not to be the victims of your bloodiest of all age's dictatorship. I want my testimonials to be heard in every part of the world. You made your own home country into a closed society, one huge concentration camp, and a gas chamber with iron curtain around the country; you turned it into a big prison for the entire nation, one giant Gulag galaxy. You made everybody paranoid, suspicious and sick as you were a huge success in that. You made everybody spy, false reports, slander and libel on each other. Brother against father, sister against mother, and son against mother. You made your spy machine watch everybody 24 hours a day, 7 days a week, 365 days a year, every year since November the 7, 1917 till December, 1991, when the Soviet Communist Empire fell apart.

You destroyed your own country, your own home, and people's lives. You turned the whole system into self-destruction and self-extermination. You made slander, libel, discrimination, disorder, anarchy and lawlessness a norm of every day. You were paranoid yourself and killed your own wife. You ordered all your rivals, competitors and opponents to be murdered, ousted, expelled, deported, expatriated and exiled. You, your entourage, your gang, your cast, your clan, your clique murdered 68, that is, sixty eight million citizens of the Soviet Union of all ethnic backgrounds during the peace time from 1924 till 1953. Plus you are accountable for the murders of about 30 million Russians during the Second World War against Nazi Germany due to signing your secret non-aggression pact with Hitler. Secretly you agreed to divide the world into spheres of influence and get your own big pie that cost the world Holocaust, devastation and millions of lives. That is how you earned your highest military rank and most honored among military titles-generalissimo. Only a few of the selected men were honored with such a title and the Victory order as the highest Russian distinction for the military deeds and feats. It is how you earned your title by sending your countrymen to death. You did not trust anybody. As soon as World War Two started, you deported to Siberia many ethnic minorities including my relatives. Night was your favorite time, your ally, your accomplice and your lover. Most people disappeared in Russia in the nighttime. After slandering, libel and false accusations, the NKVD, Russian Secret Police, arrested people and their whereabouts were not known to their relatives till the end of their lives. Typically they were murdered in the Gulag hard labor or concentration camps.

Your best friend and associate, L. Beria, NKVD chief, also loved the night. He used to hop in the "black raven," the Russian version of the sedan luxury car and hunt down pretty, sometimes teenage blonde haired ladies. Definitely, you knew well about his mortal adventures, mania, mortal addictions and obsessions and habits. He was assigned a luxurious apartment in a beautiful district of Moscow, which he kept especially for his orgies, heavy drinking, rivers of alcohol, and raping the innocent women lasted forever. You and your entourage had plenty of food when the whole nation was starving. And after many hours of orgies the young, pretty women disappeared. They were shot to death by Beria to leave no corpus delicti, no evidence of the crime, no traces. You had good lawyers they defended your destructive system, your murderers, your lawlessness and yourself. You raped the whole country you turned the whole country into one big, orgy house and a gigantic cemetery. I could not visit that wonderful place in Moscow anymore after I got to know about your friend Beria's crimes. It is like a cemetery now. You murdered intellectuals, writers, statesmen, many men, doctors and artists. You murdered my favorite writers, actors, humorists, musicians, playwrights, and performers. You murdered my nephews, my first cousins, my two little sisters, my father, you kidnapped my girlfriend and you took my wife from me. You made me a widower. You stole my childhood, my youth and you made me age in my prime time You stole my books, my library; you stole my toys and games and deprived me of my friends, and murdered my classmates. You owe me big time. You stole our Christmas and replaced it with New Year celebration in 1936. You did not allow us to have checking accounts, you did not allow us to have property or own property. You made me leave my country, lose my sweet home, my citizenship and become an émigré defector, expatriate, like other 30 million Russians who left their homeland to search for a better life. You expelled, dumped, deported and interned the cream of the crop, the intellectuals, clergy, and you deported dissenters to Siberia or expelled them to the West countries.

You recruited agents everywhere, both inside Russia and outside in every office, unit, department, division, city, region, and agency. You recruited agents to hunt down your opponents overseas. You ordered the agents to assassinate your former associates. You may want to know what has happened after March 5, 1953, when you died. Nothing in particular. A few mockeries and operetta coup d'états. Your system collapsed in December 1991. The countries of the former Soviet Federation are still in destitution and devastation with your legacy Generalissimo. The Communist system collapsed as your dream of classless society did not work. It was a bluff and nonsense. You should have tested Communism on guinea pigs, test rabbits, and first checked with animal rights activists before you made your own nation hostage and victim of your insanity, bloody and brutal.

Your country is still struggling in misery and destitution. You made us feel very unwelcome and unappreciated in our own, home country. You censored my every word and screened all my letters and private correspondence for all the years that I lived under your system. You stole my own books, the books that I wrote; you said they are the property of your government, although I am the author and the creator. You stole my own library of about two thousand books that belonged to me. The law meant nothing to you. You obstructed me; you did not allow me to be published in local or national publication in my own country.

You were paranoid and suspicious when my friends published my pieces in other countries. You could not tolerate dissent or diversity. You did not know what it was. You did not allow me to correspond with my Western friends. You did not allow me to visit the most loyal Soviet satellite country when I got the official invitation to do the research project for the dialect study. You were paranoid of everything, including local Slavic dialects. You stole my jobs, you demoted me, obstructed me, you made me unemployable, I was on your "black list" and Special Index list, made up by your suppressive secret police for those who disagreed with your system and your propaganda machine and were the first to be deported or murdered in case the war broke out. You lied to me and cheated me, you pretended you didn't see the problems. You created the problems for me, for my family, for my country, you discriminated me, you always hired and paid somebody to slander and libel me, you terminated me in violation of all possible laws. You made all my skills, all my knowledge and expertise, my multilingual, my legal, medical, educational, literary accomplishments, awards and talents unworthy, rusty, wasted and worthless. You ruined my life, you destroyed my country, and you destroyed my mom's homeland, my sisters', and my father's, my cousins' country. You owe me big time. You owe us all a big time. You owe us a country that you destroyed and stole from us. From many millions of Russians. You stole my plans, my dreams, my ideas; you turned my country into madhouse. You owe us the country. You owe us life.

No Place For a Woman

Moments are rare when women in the former Soviet Union can forget about the frustrating limits on their lives. Soviet women are very happy when they give birth and the child is a boy because they believe his life and fate will be better than a girl's would. Women don't have an easy existence in the nations that made up the Soviet Union. Sometimes it seems that the day in early March set aside for honoring them is the only time when they feel truly happy. On Women's International Day which still is widely celebrated there, husbands, sons, daughters or grandchildren present women gifts and flowers. There are lots of smiles and toasting. There are parties at restaurants and cafes. It's the day when women of all ages forget their pressing problems, their troubles, their daily hunting for bread and other necessities. But the March celebration belies the stark reality of being a woman in what was the Soviet Union.

According to the latest census, there are more than 151 million women in Russia. Although the Soviet constitution proclaimed equality of the sexes, in reality, the government contradicted the declaration. Women were not usually trusted to occupy executive posts in the state, governmental and Communist Party bodies at all levels—region, constituent republic, oblast, or federal. No Soviet woman was elected to be a member of the Politburo, the party's highest executive, policy making panel. Soviet women weren't trusted during the Soviet period, either, to enter the Moscow Institute of International Relations, MGIMO, and its academy, which trains diplomats. Foreign VIPs, sons of party bosses, and top officials from socialist countries were allowed to enter, but not the Soviet women. Exceptions to this exclusion from high level politics were rare.

One exception was the minister of culture under Nikita Khrushchev-Ekaterina Furtseva. And there was Alaexandra Kollontay, who worked in Vladimir Lenin's government as ambassador to the Scandinavian countries. She was known as the leader of the "workers' opposition," favoring the idea of genuine elections. Her views were popular with industrial workers and women. Kollontay had a prominent spot when she was a member of the Central Committee in August 1917, and the first Soviet minister of welfare. She wasn't a member of the Politburo, because it wasn't in existence at that time.

154

(This article was published on 03 29 1992, pp 1C, by The Birmingham News.)

Your Own Legacy – Monologue in Front of My Family Pictures

I like to walk into my nice, busy, sometimes messy bedroom and look at and talk to the many pictures hanging on the walls. They are my treasure, my wisdom, my teachers, my wise men and wise women, my salvation, my everything. I can stay in front of the pictures for hours and stare into faces so dear and near to me and my family. These are the pictures of immediate and extended family members, my parents and relatives, kinsmen and our family's sponsors. All these people played a role, big or small, but a good role in my life and my family's life. It is due to them, their contributions and skills, good, smart books, legacies, lessons, Purple Heart medal, talents, their support and qualifications, inventions and discoveries that I am here, that I am where I am today. Without them I would not be here. I look into their eyes and ask myself often, almost daily: "What legacy, values, skills, talents and contributions are you going to leave for your posterity?" Sometimes I feel the need to offer my apologies to my family, immediate and extended, for not spending enough time with them, for making fun of them when it was not appropriate, for not appreciating, valuing and welcoming enough their kindness, generosity, beauty, hospitality, sincerity and senses of humor. I try to read all these pictures as a family book, as an encyclopedia of the family history, genealogy, as a treasure of family traditions and history.

I learn a lot from this encyclopedic collection. I learn about their courage, determination, perseverance, unconditional love, faith, family, moral and Christian values, compassion, forgiveness, inspiration, aspiration, confidence, patience, self-preservation, survival, hard work, commitment to excellence and doing a superior job, non-compromising. Due to them, their dedication and loyalty, I have been shaped the way I am accepted and do my best to act as a civilized citizen in a civilized society.

155

"Soviet Coup of August 1991 Aborted"

The coup attempt in the Soviet Union was successfully aborted before 250,000 sets of handcuffs had been ordered by the coup masters. Apparently they expected the Soviet people to march hand in hand, in handcuffs, since 300,000 arrest orders were issued by the chief of the Moscow Military Region during the first two days of the coup attempt.

Last August 1991, the coup attempt was nothing new for most of the Soviet people, although some of them, especially intellectuals, got a real fright. Had the coup been a success, the plotters would have flooded the country with blood in the most atrocious Stalin-Yezhov-Beria style.

Obviously, reasonable people should have been frightened because of 300,000 arrest orders by the chief of the Moscow Military Region in first days of the putsch, and the order for 250,000 pairs of handcuffs which went out from a trading company situated at the telephone apparatus factory somewhere in the provinces near Moscow. Ex-KGB chief, Vladimir Kryuchkov, by coded telegram ordered all units of the national, Republic and local as well as related organizations and frontier guards which are affiliated with the KGB, to go on "top alert," a status which usually has meant "undeclared war" or "civil war." KGB officers were offered double salaries and bonuses in August. Although the coup only lasted 72 hours, the plotters were very optimistic, energetic, open to the point of being impudent, confident and abusive to the people of the USSR. But if the plotters had succeeded, it would have meant a bloodbath with reprisals as in 1937.

Within the USSR, the coup was referred to by the old fascist German term "putsch" because the plotters were viewed by the bulk of the population as fascists who wanted to push the country over the edge into the abyss. Ironically enough, the country had already been in the abyss for some time. Still, the coup was like something from an operetta; it failed because it was not professionally conducted and well done. But it never could have succeeded anyway because it would have had to face strong international isolation, sanctions, freezing of technical and financial aid from the West, as well as opposition from inside the USSR.

The Soviet people don't believe in much of anything anymore; they are awfully afraid of changes and altered expectations; after 73 years of Communist dictatorship, they are simply "fearful." With the

156

recent collapse of the national economy, its industry and agriculture, the majority of people are poor and they didn't expect that anything like a coup could happen at all. Soviet people today live in an atmosphere of psycho-neuroticism, hatred, daily strain and fright, a high tenseness. Irrespective of their social, religious, ethnic or economic position, certain madness and stupor characterize them, so that the country looks like a mental hospital. The cracking up of the Soviet empire makes today a troublesome period of history, and the country looks like a transit train station or the waiting room of an international airport. The most of would be passengers were waiting for days, months and even up to one year to buy tickets and board the international airliners that fly out once or twice a week. In fact, I was at Moscow's international airport, Sheremetyevo-1 recently and had been there sixteen months before. On the earlier occasion, I saw long lines of smiling and laughing foreign tourists, business people and Soviet officials well dressed, serious and cone VIPs, checking in for international flights. Then in September, after the coup attempt, I saw long lines there again, but the atmosphere was gloomy and so sad that the building itself seemed to be not so well-lit. The travelers were not so luxuriously clad this time, they did not smile, they were far too serious to smile or to laugh. There were Jews, Georgians, Armenians and ethnic Germans of different ages, with pieces of luggage, waiting for many days, checking their names on the list for the two weekly Aeroflot flights to New York. They clutched their letters from the Immigration and Naturalization Service of the US State Department, for which they have had to wait many months and years to be placed in the annual quota of Soviet Jews to move to the USA, In several hours, they will become Soviet émigrés—and American immigrants.

Meanwhile, people in America speak of forthcoming hunger in the USSR, possible pogroms. The notorious organization "Pamyat" (a word which means "memory" but very short memory) calls itself historical and patriotic but it is in reality chauvinistic, anti-Semitic and nationalistic. "It has strict rules: the entrance fee to the organization is to provide home addresses and phone numbers of two Jewish families in the USSR. Pamyat was allowed to hold its rally on Red Square in Moscow two years ago, something which had never before been allowed. The society publishes a newspaper which was not registered under the Soviet law. It looks like the Soviet Government and its protégés and patrons were comfortable with the Pamyat status and acquiesced with the notorious actions and activities. We, likewise, waited at the airport for fourteen hours. We wanted to put our toddler in the baby room, but it turns out that they have only mother's and children's rooms there with only two baby beds and armchairs for all those people. So my son and I had to doze and keep watch on our luggage. We talked with a young family of Soviet ethnic Germans with a baby. The father told me that they came from a district near Tashkent, capital of Uzbekistan. They got a private invitation from friends in Germany, FRG, .i.e. Federal Republic of Germany, to visit. They wanted to immigrate, but the procedure of arranging formalities for their emigration is complicated and takes too much time. Moreover, they ran into problems with OVIR, the notorious Soviet visa and registration service, which was unwilling or reluctant to perform its duties because of the mass emigration now happening in the USSR. The father had to bribe OVIR employee 1,000 rubles, and then pay an additional 1,000 rubles, the newly accepted price for a foreign travel Soviet passport. All this did help. The family will go to Germany and there ask the Immigration and Naturalization Service for permanent residence and German citizenship. In Russian, this means defecting.

My friends from the USA have sent me newspaper clippings which printed the draft Soviet legislation on freedom of travel and emigration. This new law, so long expected, will come into effect in January 1993, all my friends were confused into believing it took effect in 1992. How? One should ask the Soviet people if they feel free to travel since the 1991 session of the Soviet parliament adopted that long disputed and twice cancelled bill on freedom of travel. Remember that the USSR did not ratify the Universal Declaration on Human Rights which stipulates freedom of travel and free passage, freedom to choose a residence or domicile in any country of the world. Not for Soviet people. People are free to travel from one office to another and to prepare heaps of stupid and unnecessary documents and papers, to sign them, seal them, to redo them and start all over again and wait in long lines for many, many months to get permission merely to visit friends or relatives abroad. And, even if they raise the necessary sums of money and spend six months killing time with OVIR, they may then be told that there are no passport forms available. Since adoption of the travel permits in May 1991, almost 200,000 Soviet Jews have been refused permission to emigrate to Israel and other foreign, mainly Western, countries until they change their Soviet exit visas into foreign travel passports, which

158

automatically means the loss of Soviet citizenship. (Some people call this the anti-Jewish Chernobyl.) Since 1967, when the USSR broke diplomatic relations with Israel, Soviet Jews automatically lose their Soviet citizenship after moving to Israel. There was recently an appeal by six intellectuals in the Russian Republic, including the prominent writer Valentin Rasputin, calling upon the Soviet official bodies to ban emigration of Soviet Jews because the Soviet state needs their brains, their capabilities, their industriousness, but also because Jews were blamed for some of the tragedies resulting from the Bolshevik revolution. Issuing domestic and foreign travel passports to Soviet Jews would mean that they would have a chance to change their opinion about migration and to return home if they dislike the new country or the new lifestyle. At the same time, it means that Soviet Jews would be looking for a job and better life while continuing to be Soviet citizens and a sort of "gast-arbeiters" or guest workers abroad, paying dues, fees, taxes. Thus, Soviet procedures can last from several weeks to several months. And if a person doesn't have an invitation from a foreign country, then one's only option to go abroad is as a tourist, but only if you have hard foreign currency. That is particularly true for travel to Western countries.

If, however, one has a contract or employment at, let us say, the University Russian Research Center, one will be told that contracts are not arranged by the notorious OVIR, Visa Issuance & Regulations Department, but by the visa committee which was, until recently, a section of the Soviet Communist Party Regional Committee, officially run by the Soviet KGB that controlled all spheres of Soviet life, including screening, scanning, vetting, endorsement and approval and issuance of exit Soviet visas and entrance visas to foreigners and Russians. Now it is a section of the Regional Executive Committee in the same imposing building, and the same person who has run it the past several years as chief of the Communist Party, now runs it by occupying the position of the chairman of the Regional Executive Committee. They are open only three working hours per day, three working days per week (a little bit more at OVIR.) And here one will be told that your contract is private, official, it is your private business and that means you cannot go abroad because only official travel may be authorized.

Such is the freedom of travel in the Soviet style. Lawyers will not help you because you belong to the system and they defend the system.

This article was written in October 1991 and published by the
B*irmingham News.*

The Status of Religion in the USSR

*"The Communist Party cannot be neutral toward religion. It stands for
science, and all religion is opposed to science."*

Joseph Stali

The 1917 Bolshevik revolution nationalized all propertie
belonging to religious entities, an action aimed at ending thei
educational and philanthropic activities and significantly reducing thei
political influence in Russia.

From the very first days of its existence, the Soviet state declare
its antipathy and hostility towards religion and God believers in Russi
and later in the USSR. Atheism was the Soviet government's officia
doctrine and policy and a mandatory subject at schools of all levels
Attacks on believers were considered to be part of a daily functioning o
the Soviet society. The November 2, 1917, Declaration of the Rights o
the Peoples of Russia abolished all national religious privileges an
restrictions, aimed at the Russian Orthodox Church, the state church o
the tsarist regime. Other decrees gave Russia's Commissariat o
Education the authority over church schools and teaching institutions
only civil marriages were recognized to be legal and state funding o
churches was cut. Per the 1918 Russian Constitution, the clergy wer
stripped off their constitutional rights and condemned along with ex
police force, criminals and capitalists, and were deprived of their right
to vote and hold office.

The state and religion were firmly separated. Special ordinance
identified churches and cults such as Russian Orthodox, Old Believers
Georgian, Catholic and Protestants (all as one). Judaism, Buddhism an
Islam were not listed at all. The Bolshevik Party Congresses, as early a
1919 and 1921, adopted an aggressive program of scientific anti
religious propaganda. The Bolshevik Party seized church possession
during the 1922 famine to satisfy the emergency needs which intensifie
the struggle**.** Abuses, executions, including of the Metropolitan o
Petrograd, large scale anti-religious propaganda and official criticism
campaign, assault on religion, zealous, abusive atheism, closings of th

houses of prayer, disruption of the worship services, searches of the priests, imprisonments, intimidations and harassments of the clergy became the norms of life and modus operandi of the new Bolshevik government. In 1921, teaching of religion was restricted only to the seminaries and in 1924, only to homeschooling. In 1929, the Soviet stat, amidst the so called *"class struggle with the enemy elements"* officially tightened the officially declared control of state over religion: religious groups and societies had to be registered with the state and were restricted only to religious activities, funds could be raised only within the same groups and not outside the groups as fee charges; meetings and worship services to be held only on the state licensed premises and registered buildings, rented from the Soviet government with a special permission and charities were not allowed. All this business was run by the notorious, punitive NKVD-type Soviet government agency, called "The USSR Council on Religious Affairs and Cults." The 1936 Stalin Constitution outlawed Christmas and replaced it with the New Year celebration and declared the right to profess the religion, but not to propagate it, which confined the believers to the status of "the closet believers."

The huge place of worship, very popular not only with Muscovites, but all Russians, Christ the Savior Cathedral in Moscow, as part of Stalin's blood thirsty dictatorship and paranoia of seeing enemies and spies in every corner of his Stalinland, Stalin ordered the same church to be destroyed. Here are devastating statistics: in 1953 there were 15,000 churches in USSR which were significantly reduced to 6,794 by 1986. It is believed that there were 1,312 mosques served by 8,052 mullahs in the entire USSR with reported deportations of Muslims from the Caucasus during World War II as part of Stalin's paranoia and distrust of ethnic minorities and their religious affiliations. While Hitler's Wehrmacht machine invading Russia at the beginning of the WW II, several million believers and thousands of clergymen were arrested and many more deported; all monasteries and seminaries and other places of worship were forcibly closed and centralized ecclesiastical administration ceased to exist.

The poignant history of the banned Ukrainian Unitarian Church is the testament of the Soviet communist brutal policies with thousands of obstinate adherents were deported, four million underground with masses in forests and cellars. Persecutions, beatings of the church members, disruption of the Christmas celebrations (on January 6) were reported and the churches were blocked by the Soviet police who tried to force the Orthodox priests to take services. As we see, the most popular words that came into being with the Bolshevik government were "restrictions," "deportations," "force" and "executions" and "expropriations."

In spite of the hostility that the official Soviet authorities displayed daily towards the believers in Russia, religion, belief in God and God's word were strong and everlasting, never-ending. My parents like many other Christians in Russia, had to become closet Christians after the Soviet authorities shut down our village church early in 1960s but my parents kept observing all the Russian Orthodox religious holidays, feasts, and traditions and kept praying daily.

I was always bothered by this question: Why were the Soviet Government and society so hostile and hateful to religion and to believers and Christians in the USSR? Why did the government disrespect God and why did they always attack the God believers and destroy many churches and executed and murdered many priests and clergymen?

Another big adjustment for me in America was the freedom of religion. The Russians declared freedom of religion but in reality it did not exist. When we came to this country, there were so many churches. So many religions in the USA! In Odessa, a city of million citizens, there were only four churches. One was the synagogue. As local tour guides, we were not allowed by the instructions of our travel service bosses to disclose the location of the synagogue in Odessa due to Anti-Semitism and break=up of the Soviet-Israeli official and diplomatic relations. Definitely there was a significant number of Western and foreign visitors of Jewish descent and inquired and wanted to visit the synagogue in Odessa.

Soviet Constitution – The Most Fraudulent Document of the Century

Why did the USSR not sign the *Universal Declaration of Human Rights*? What is the reason the Soviet Union, being one of the five charter members of the United Nations (in 1945) has chosen deliberately not to sign the *Universal Declaration of Human Rights,* adopted by the

162

United Nations Organization's General Assembly in 1948? Because the USSR, the Soviet communist system and the Soviet government were dictatorial, authoritarian, and self-destructive regimes. Read all thirty articles and the preamble of the *Universal Declaration of Human Rights* and you will see that the USSR violated most or all of them, which is why the USSR did not want to sign it, because the USSR turned its own country into one big house, one big prison for the Soviet people, as it was actually unofficially called in the USSR. *Right to freedom and liberty, freedom of thought, conscience, religion, opinion, expression, peaceful assembly, take part in the government, to own property not in the USSR. The Communists suppressed it all.*

Everyone has the right to leave the country including his own and to return to his own country; Everyone has the right to seek and enjoy in other countries asylum from persecution—not in the USSR. You did not have those rights.

My First Alma Mater, Krinichnoyeh High School

My Welcoming Address to My Alma Mater on the 170th Anniversary of the Foundation of Krinichnoyeh School
Dear Teachers, Staff members, Administration of Krinichnoyeh High School, the residents of the village of Krinichnoyeh and esteemed guests:

My heartfelt congratulations on the 170th anniversary of the foundation of our alma mater, Krinichnoyeh School and 50th anniversary of establishing the high school in the village of Cheshma Varovita, now Krinichnoeyh.

I am very proud of your success and achievements of our alma mater, our native, mother school and of the invaluable contributions that you, all our teachers of our school, made.

I am proud to be the graduate of Krinichnoyeh High School, our alma mater, the key word of which "mater" in Latin means "mother," the school, whose teachers, administration and the staff members displayed motherly and fatherly love towards us, students.
In the long list of the schools, institutes, colleges, universities that I attended, went to, graduated from, associated myself with and taught classes and seminars in, the name of my school, the name of Krinichnoyeh High School, proudly occupies the first line and is written and inscribed with golden letters.

Thank you very much for that great wealth of knowledge and your invaluable investment in us, our education and our future. Knowledge is power at all times. It is the power of your motherly and fatherly care, support and love that you constantly granted to us. It is the power that carried us throughout the turbulent years in our lives. This is the power of education that nobody will take away from us, this is the warranty and the power that never abandoned me.

My heartfelt gratitude and admiration go to you for your heroic, teachers' job well done. I wish you all good health, great success, peace and all the best.

Yours,

Peter Kirchikov

Letter to My Mother

My very dearest mom in the world,

Sorry, I did not write you for so long. It has been twenty one years since we saw each other last time in your home. Actually, this is my first letter since I immigrated with my family to this country. I could not imagine that we would become émigrés, political immigrants, a status that is not known to many local people.

We became stateless, people without passports and with no citizenship. Could you imagine, that twenty one years after our bitter and severe separation from the country of our origin, I would be writing this letter to you in English, not in my mother tongue, not in my native language, sweet Southern Slavic dialect, that is known for its old church Slavonic language origin, for the greatest contribution to the world classic and modem literature? I did not know life would be so unfair, that we would not be able to see each other for such a long period and maybe till the end of our days.

I don't believe it when people say, life is unfair. I believe that people and politicians make life unfair and miserable. Life is a great gift full of blessings and happiness. We could not believe that the worst nuclear tragedy in Chernobyl, Ukraine, two hundred miles away from your home, could happen in April 1986. The ecocide took thousands and thousands of lives in our home country and still continues to kill people of all ages and will unfortunately destroy many more lives in the future. You remember my second son, Maxim. He was eleven months old when the nuclear fallout struck. He died of leukemia in July 1989. You could not imagine there would be so many losses and deaths in our family that would affect our lives so much. You could not imagine that your two little daughters, ages 3 and 4 years, our two sisters, would die during the horrible starvation in Ukraine in 1946, a year after devastating World War II. We never saw our little sisters. They died after they ate the oil sunflower cake, the only food item that was available in the family and the community there at that time. The oil cake, typically fed to the animals, was for them like Hershey's, Reese's or brownies for our kids here. Our father was out of town, trying to sell some farmer's products to make some money in that hard time to make ends meet and save the family. When he got to know about the loss of his two daughters, he bought candies and gave them to the kids at the major train station where he first learned about the terrible news. His eyes were full of tears, his heart was bleeding. We never saw our two sisters because they died before we were born. There are no perfect societies and accidents can happen in the best of families. But you could not believe that in the 21st century human values, moral values, human life, worthiness, trust, proficiency, professionalism, expertise, experience, skills, talents, excellence, dedication, commitment, sometimes, at certain places, will be wasted all the way to the utmost and will not be valued at all, neglected, wasted, dumped and destroyed.

Yes, Mom, I am happy in my new home. No, I will never forget my real mother, you, Mom, for the rest of my life. I will never forget the place, the country where I was born and grew up, where I was educated, trained and played soccer, volleyball and basketball. I will never forget my friends, relatives, teachers, mentors, coaches. I will always remember your beef stew, feta cheese, sour cream soup with cabbage borsch. I will never forget your lessons of hard, smart, diligent, honest, dedicated work. I know how hard you and daddy had to work all your lives to make your living. You were 5 years old when you were hired by the rich family to work as a baby sitter, a maid and a house worker to get some food on the family table in exchange of your almost twelve hours, seven day per week in an undeveloped country, equivalent to the third world poverty states.

You both had to work hard to survive because you could not rel on a regular supply of ordinary goods and commodities. You had to b self-sufficient because the government and the system did not care mucl about the people in the country. You could not buy potato chips, Frencl fries or chewing gum. Owning US dollars or other Western fre convertible currency was a criminal offense for almost seventy thre years. You had to work so hard to put my sister and me through colleg and to help my older brother get trade and occupation in his life. Th hardest thing was to take care of your health problems in the communit where almost no health care or first aid was available. You told me you loved me most of all in the world and I feel I am the happiest man in th world. When I was growing up, when I was going to school and t college, you always asked: "My dearest son, please promise me, afte you graduate, you will stay with us, you will never leave us, you wil never leave your mother's home, your family nest, your mother' homeland. I will be the happiest granny and I will take care of you family after you marry a real Southern, real blonde, witty beauty and will babysit your many children twenty four hours a day. You don't hav to pay me anything just a cup of hot tea and a bowlful of grapes wil carry me through the day. Will you promise me that?"

Yes, Mom, I did promise you that. You asked me that man times when I visited your home and I promised you always to stay witl you. You also wanted me to major in medicine, not in English. You considered that to be practical. You and daddy wanted me to be medical doctor to cure you from all known and unknown diseases and illnesses, that Soviet medicine could not help arthritis, diabete rheumatism, high blood pressure. I did promise you to become an MD Sorry, Mom, I broke my promises, I did not become a medical doctor t treat you and daddy from your excruciating and killing pains and diseases. I did not mean to do that. Instead, I became a rebel and maverick in our community. I did not stay with you and daddy for th rest of my life. Instead, my family and I found ourselves overseas, te thousand miles away from you and our native place. Sorry, Mom, I di not realize some diseases could be treacherous and cost us life and tha some people take advantage of peoples' illnesses, provoke ill people and try to benefit from their infirmities. I didn't know that would be a popula profession of the 21st century and a profitable, bloody business. I knov there are various laws in the world such as family, international corporate, real estate, divorce, immigration, copyright, acquisition, civil rights laws. There are no perfect laws. There are laws that may destroy your life or degrade, or make you miserable for the rest of your life. But we know what is right and what is wrong. We know that honesty, integrity, fairness, loyalty, justice and history are the best judges.

Yes, Mom, you asked me about Easter. I am having a great time here in the USA where egg hunting is a big tradition here, like egg dying over there in my native place. But I will always miss you, Paskha, the Easter cake, sweet, brown-reddish bread, Easter party and "Christos Voskres!" "Voistinu Voskres!" "Christ is Risen!" "He is risen indeed!'"

Where are you, Mom, now? Are you still waiting for me to come home? Is your borsch-soup with cabbage and sour cream ready? Is it still hot or cold? Latecomers always get the cold meal, we learned the lesson. I miss you and I love you much. I did not realize that the feelings could mean so much to me and overpower me. My love for you is overwhelming. I see you everywhere, although at your eighty five now you can hardly walk around your house or the front and back yard, using your manmade cane of a twig. I sent you two metal folding canes one for you and one for Daddy. Daddy used his cane until the brutal disease took him away from us in a very cruel way. You never got used to your metal cane. Most of the time we spent together with you were working, trying to make both ends meet, to bring some food to the table. We worked in our kitchen yard, in the vineyard, digging the windlass well or we worked in the collective farm and in the farm fields. You said you were proud of how you raised us and proud of our accomplishments. You said you wanted us to inherit long lasting values and love our families above all. I am glad we were loyal and true to your legacy and expectations. But you did not expect me to become an immigrant and live 10,000 miles away from you. You never left the community where you grew up. You never left the village.

You never traveled to big cities like we did. You don't have the faintest idea what a foreign country is and what it looks like. I wish you could see for yourself how beautiful America is. Now you know, first hand, well how visa and visa saga and visa arrangements could separate and destroy families and what the test of patience and survival means. You did not know much about green cards, permanent residency, relative's petition, immigration and naturalization until we came to this country. Now you know it well. My dearest mom, I will always

remember your lovely folk and ethnic Southern Slavic songs. You voice, your songs had very special messages. I wish I could have tape your songs and your voice. Your songs are my life, my strength, m inspiration, they are predictions, they are treasured values, excellenc my struggle. Your songs carried me through all my life. Your song saved my life so many times. I never told you about this. I wish I cou have shared with you while you are still alive--you deserve a great cred for your songs. Your songs helped me not to compromise, never to giv up, never to surrender. Your songs are my guidelines, lighthouse an search light, they were a bright light in darkness, a sunshine on a gloom nasty day. I will always be indebted to you, Mom, till the end of th world. I miss your songs greatly, Mom. I miss you, Mom, greatly. Wher are you now, Mom? Can you hear me? Can you sing me a song of th five hundred year suppression history of the country where our ancesto came from and the beautiful girl waiting for the true liberators of th nation to come? Are you sleeping well at night or is arthritis is sti bothering you as it was many years ago? Do condroitin and glucosamin that I sent help you now? Are you still alive? I wish I could sing you songs. Wait for me and I will write you another letter. Wait for me and will come to see you. Wait for me patiently and tenderly and certainly will come home. There is no way to measure my love to you, Mom!
Much love,
Your son,
Expatriate, émigré.
Peter

Sovietspeak

Glossary of Soviet-Era Terms

Apparat Communist bureaucratic machine of professional party employees and office holders controlling all sectors and spheres of the Soviet life.

Apparatchik Communist party and government official, full-time well-paid bureaucrat who makes his/her living by promoting and enforcing the ideology and doctrines of Marxism-Leninism and CPSU.

Avos'ka Russian net and mesh shopping bag that everybody used in the USSR to shop 24/7/365, and wait in lines. Many Russians carried avos'kas with them daily in their pockets, purses, shoulder bags, ready to pull out avos'ka and shop. Avos'kas became the unforgettable symbol of the total failure of the Communist economic and political mismanagement system that led to the collapse of the Soviet empire.

AKTIV 1. Communist Party Active -- decision-making body
2. Volunteers -- well-screened and trained by the Communist party and the KGB who passed all background and loyalty checks. Also: free-lance interpreters, activists, trained to debate with Western visitors and were considered to be patriots. The "Aktiv" people were the Soviet Communist ideological SWAT team.

Artel a cooperative of workers or peasants farmers, industrial or agricultural workers under the supervision of the government. Collective farms were types of artels started in 1929 after the Soviet Communist Party's 16th Congress that signaled the forced collectivization and nationalization of the agriculture, spearheaded by Dictator Stalin. In this context it is the agricultural producers' cooperative enterprise. Initially they were industrial cooperatives among itinerant workers, but later were extended to collective farms and artisan's artels.

April 1986 Chernobyl Nuclear Disaster, USSR's national tragedy and major environmental ecocide, of nuclear fall-out at the Chernobyl nuclear power plant on April 26, 1986. Chernobyl is less than a hundred kilometers from Kiev, the Ukraine's major city and about four hundred kilometers away from Odessa, the city where we lived.

Blat pull, clout, having influential friends, powerful mentors and fathers in powerful offices to take care of you, your family, your life, career; corruption, 'blat" penetrated all areas of Soviet life. Bribery was part of the "blat" and expected everywhere in every office, with the police, the government, schools, doctors' offices, and corruption, for promotion, for a pay raise, for bonus, to doctors, police, and predatory seduction. Blat: Soviet communist cronyism, Lenin-Stalin legacy of Soviet favoritism, protection, pull, protection, cronyism and illegal, illegitimate, unlawful pulling of strings. Gaining, obtaining, deriving favors, services, goods, promotion, bonuses, upgrading your status, position, reputation, posture, economic, political, social, family position, status due to or through employment of the tactics and strategies of bribery, solicited or unsolicited gifts, presents, entertainment, returned favors, services, under-the counter-exchange, behind-the scene-machinations, deals, operations, manipulations, decisions, influences, and impacts. Blat- the never-ending legacy was and still is the king in Russia and former Soviet countries. The Soviet Union is dead, long live the king!

Bolshevik - same as Communist.

Chistka mass executions, associated with Stalin's Great Terror and "Great Purges" of 1936-1938, mass terror of the Soviet Communist party members, armed forces personnel, police force, intelligence service, military intelligence, media, reporters, writers, professionals, show biz people, entertainers, actors, common people, clerical personnel, removal and elimination of hostile party elements.

By stating **"Cadres decide everything,"** Dictator Stalin meant that the Soviet Communist personnel departments at all levels were empowered to make all decisions to implement Stalin's Communist doctrines and ideals into life. However, there was a serious counteraction to Stalin's action "Cadres decide everything" as a new powerful to oppose Stalin's directive: *"Stay away from the personnel department—go around it in* *thousand miles. Fear it like a hell, like a high-rise building fire.*" This saying was a proof of resistance to Dictator Stalin.

CEMA/COMECON Council for Mutual Economic Assistance. Russian for: SEV—Soviet Ekonomicheskoi Vzaimoposhchi...

CCCP - Russian for the USSR- stands for Souyuz Sovetskih Sotsialisticheskih Respublik.

CC - Central Committee of the CPSU.

Collective Farms or Kolkhoz - Agricultural Artel - the term "artel" dates back to the 19th century when in it was popular in Russia for associations of independent laborers to get united for collective work with division and sharing the profit and liability. The origin is Russian "Артель"--came into use in 1884-- "Artel" via Italian –*"artieri"* plural— "artisans", *"artier"*-artisan', via Latin –*"ars"*—art.

CPSU - CC, CPSU, Central Committee, Communist Party of the USSR.

Dekulakization, "raskulachivanie," Stalin's decreed dispossession, elimination of well-to-do Russian farmers. Between five and ten million people died due to the Stalin's destruction of kulaks that resulted in Stalin's man-made famine due to the disruption of the Soviet agriculture especially in the Ukraine the process of "dekulakization," elimination of kulaks as the class in the USSR by Stalin in the 1930s. Kulaks and their families were deported to Siberia and forced to settle in the frigid, subfreezing conditions. Kulaks were deprived and plundered of their private property and any and all ownership.

DUMA - the lower house of the tsarist legislature, created in October 1905. The upper house consisted of the Provisional Government. In today's Russia: DUMA is the Russian Federation's parliament.

"Iron" Felix Dzerzhinsky - highly idolized by the KGB clan, the chief and founder of the VCHK, the Russian Soviet Bolshevik Secret service, counterintelligence and espionage agency to combat the counter-revolutionary and counterespionage and subversive activities.

GULAG, Glavnoye Upravlenie Lagerei - Chief Administration of Corrective Labor Camps and Settlements, a function of the KGB running a wide network of prison and hard labor camps; epitome of the USSR's penal system. "The Gulag Archipelago" by Alexander Solzhenitsyn and other his writings made the GULAG Soviet penitentiary system of hard labor and prison camps notorious all over the world with its millions of victims and epitome of the Soviet atrocious Stalinist dictatorial regime.

 "Harakteristika" - literal translation: "Character profile, summary of the character, personal and professional skills and qualifications and experience." The official reference letter in lieu of a personal CV or resume as it is in this country: the reference becomes part of your official file in your personnel records with four mandatory signatures: by the boss of the Communist party local division; by the boss, your company General manager; by the trade union boss, by the AYCL boss, All Union Young Communist Leninist League.

Helsinki Accord - Human Rights Final Agreement signed in Helsinki in 1975.

Helsinki Groups, or Helsinki Watch Groups - founded in 1975 and 1976 in several cities in the USSR to monitor the compliance of the Soviet Communist authorities with the Helsinki Accord, The Human Rights Final Agreement. Their goals were to secure and further the rights of would-be Soviet emigrants of the ethnic Jews, Germans and less to Armenians and to encourage disarmament.

Internment Camps in the USSR – see also: to intern: vt: **(1866)** - to confine or impound, especially during wartime, enemies, aliens, anti-Soviet elements, political, religious dissidents, Soviet citizens who were captured by Nazi Germany as WW II prisoners of war **; internee;** The USSR's government, especially under Lenin and Stalin ordered internment, deportation and detention during the civil war 1918-1922, in 1930s, before WW II and after the WW II, as part of "The Return to the

Motherland" of the Soviet or former Soviet citizens, including the WW II captives, POWs, prisoners of war captured by Nazi Germany's and its allies. The USSR's government, ordered internment, deportation, and detention also including the ethnic groups hated and distrusted by the Stalin murder machine: ethnic Germans, ethnic Tartars, Jews, and Bulgarians. Stalin distrusted them and was confident they would betray him during the Nazi Germany's invasion of the USSR. There were different categories of internees and detainees that were thrown into the Soviet Gulag prison camps settlements. Some of the internees were imprisoned for being accused of being disloyal to the Soviet motherland, for anti-Soviet propaganda, for treasons or being spies of Western countries due to the Stalin's unlimited paranoia.

Iron Curtain, Iron Curtain Country, the USSR - impenetrable, unbearable barrier to communication, marked by severe, brutal censorship and isolation, total control of media, arts, literature, all aspects of political, economic, private life and complete lack of freedoms and liberties. USSR, China, and North Korea. Term used by Sir Winston Churchill referring to separation between the USSR and Western countries that officially started "the cold war." Prevention of free flow of communications and people from the USSR and its allies in Eastern Europe, boundaries, frontier barriers and restrictive policies (i.e. political censorship of news of the USSR.) The term was first used by H.G. Wells in the "Food of Gods" in 1904, i.e., an enforced break of communication with society by individual. The present use since 1946 is of major "Cold War" terms, originally by Sir Vincent Troubridge.

Kolkhoz, or Collective Farm - a result of the USSR's forced mass collectivization program, begun by Stalin in 1929, which grew the number of collectivized peasants from 1.7 percent to 90 percent in 1936. Per Soviet law, the **Kolkhoz, or Collective Farm** was defined as "… *voluntary cooperative whose members pooled their means of production in order to produce in common. Members ran their own affairs and elected their management committee."* The big problem was that the kolkhoz, like everything in the USSR, was run, controlled and dictated by the CPSA, the Communist Party of the USSR, in this case by a powerful network of local, district, regional, and ethnic republic's Communist Party offices. In real life, the residents of the rural areas did not have any alternative or any other types of employment or job opportunities, except the monopoly of the Kolkhoz, Collective Farm. There were no other companies, cooperatives or job opportunities and private and free enterprise were outlawed by the Soviet laws. Two thirds of the produce went either directly as the procurement to the state or to the MTS, Machine Tractor Stations.

Kolkhozniks - members of the collective farm, were paid per their trudoden, workday units, whose quotas were heavily enforced by the Kolkhoz, or Collective Farm management.

Kulaks, well-to-do farmer, Stalin had many of the kulaks deported, interned and transported to the remote collective farms in distant places and deported to work in the agricultural labor camps. It is estimated that one in five of these deportees died, many of them were children and women. Their lives were ruined, their property, machinery, savings, equipment were lost and misappropriated by the Stalin Government. In responses to forced collectivization, many peasants offered a resistance and armed themselves against Bolsheviks.

Mud Bricks - Mud bricks were used typically for private house construction, renovation and repair of the houses in our community. Mud bricks were made out of mud, dirt that was brought from the landfill.

Muzhik, hilly-billy, a derogatory term for a simpleton, collective farmer

Nomenklatura - a list of the government posts in which appointment required party approval and reelected to similar posts or higher in other parts of the country, as they went through "good ole buddy" cronyism system. During the Brezhnev era there were two million nomenklatura members comprising very influential class that enjoyed lavish lifestyle.

"Operation Keelhaul" Forced Repatriation joined by Allied Powers. Shiploads of WWII prisoners of war, Russians, former Soviet citizens, fighting for their freedom, lives, and fear of deportation, so called "repatriation to their Russian motherland" that would execute them in Stalin's Gulag camps. "Keelhaul- "to haul a person through the water under the keel of a ship from side to side… a method of refined, inventive torture" - Webster's Dictionary.

OVIR - Otdel Viz I Registrazii, the Visa and Registration Department of the USSR's Interior Ministry Federal Police Force Department) in charge of scanning, screening, vetting, investigation, issuance, denial, rejection of all types of visas to Soviet citizens and foreigners, notorious for obstructing the justice and multiple violations of international human rights including but not limited to: the rights to passage, travel abroad, discrimination, Anti-Semitism, freedom of speech.

Otkaznik - Russian word for "refusnik" which has the same meaning. See "refusnik."

Peaceful coexistence between the Soviet orbit countries and the Western counterparts - slogan promoted by the CPSU& Soviet Government.

Pioner - pioneer, i.e. Russian Boy Scouts and Girl Scouts.

Pogrom - mass bloodshed, massacre mainly against Jewish ethnic population deeply rooted in the government-sponsored and openly supported Anti-Semitism, Judophobia and discrimination of Jews in Imperial Russia and in the USSR

Proletariat, Latin, "Proletarius" - citizen of the lowest class; working class; wage earners.

"Proletarians of all countries, unite!" - CPSU's slogan that was printed in every Soviet newspaper, magazine and the posters with this slogan everywhere seventy four years of the Soviet regime..

Propiska – "dwelling permit" from the local government, with domestic passport, that did not give you a permission to travel abroad or escape from the USSR. You could not get the passport without "blat," bribing and connections. The Soviet home passport with "propiska" served also as:

1. I.D.
2.going to the Marriage Office to sign a marriage contract
3. Visiting the "closed Soviet cities," defense industry, where foreigners were prohibited
4. Child birth and proof of parenthood, new-born baby registration,
5. Applying for Soviet foreign travel passport- You will not be allowed to move at your free will--you needed that magic "propiska", "dwelling permit" from the local government with your domestic passport,.

Refusniks, citizens, mainly of Jewish origin, who were refused Soviet exit visas to emigrate to Western countries due to their human rights activities and being labeled as dissidents. "Otkaznik" is Russian for "refusnik."

Russia same as USSR

Sovietese Soviet Lexion of the Soviet officialese, governmentalese, bureaucratese, Sovietspeak, Leninese, Stalinese.

Sovkhoz state farms, staffed and managed by the paid workers and served as models for farming methods for the peasants. In 1940 there were 400 Sovkhozes and in 1962, approximately 8,500. Sovkhoz was considered to be ideologically more advantageous to the kolkhoz as the best Soviet model of socializing agriculture.

Sputnik 1. Soviet satellite that orbited the earth in 1957, pride of the USSR. 2. Name of the International Youth Travel Bureau in the USSR.

"The 1956 Secret Speech" - by Russian Premier and Communist Chief Nikita Khrushchev re: destalinization and denunciation of Stalin's cult of personality, made at the 20th CPSU Party Congress.

"The revolution from above" Bolshevik's slogan. The revolution comes from the masses, not from the orders of the party grass-roots

Tolkach, facilitator, promoter, who pushes on behalf of his company, cronies, to promote the common cause whose job is to persuade that decision-makers to make a favorable decision that will benefit tolkach.

Tovarishch - Comrade—typical, official address in the USSR in Russian

Trudoden, work-day unit for collective farmer. Quotas were imposed on farmers and the records of trudoden per year were kept strictly and not meeting the quotas cold cause serious problems up to imprisonment. If the record was inaccurate, which was normal for the communist system, and the farmer was falsely accused of not meeting the quotas, not many remedies were available, because most of the collective farmers, like my parents, were illiterate and could not read and defend themselves. They would call on their children to fight for them.

Vozhd Russian for leader. Stalin and Lenin were called "the vozhd of all the peoples of the USSR."

155 Nationalities of the USSR - more than 155 ethnic groups, minorities mistakenly called in Russian as 155 nationalities. There was only nationality—Soviet.

9th of May - Victory in Europe Day - a holiday celebrated in the USSR.

Warsaw Pact Treaty military bloc of the Soviet satellite countries.

War Communism the policy adopted by the Lenin government during the civil war in Russia in 1917-1921, forcing the peasants to surrender all their goods, grains, staples, products, because Lenin, Bolsheviks, dictators and tyrants said so. In reality it was expropriation, plunder and robbery of the Russian peasants and farmers.

White Guard; White Movement, anti-Bolshevik armed forces that opposed Bolshevik Revolution in the civil war Why White Guard" 1. "white" vs. Red Army, and Bolshevik government, 2. White color Army uniforms of Imperial Russia

Glossary of Translation, Interpretation and Linguistic Terminology

Atril - computer program, publisher of Déjà vu.

Certified Translator-Interpreter-registered foreign language interpreter who has completed AOC/Administrative Office of Courts certification requirements.

Accredited Translator-accreditation from either ATA, American Translator's Association or ITI, International Translators Institute

A Language-mother tongue or native language.

B Language-a language that a translator is proficient enough in reading, speaking and writing comparable to A or native language that s/he can translate into or out of it.

C Language-translator can understand and read well enough to translate out of it, but cannot write, speak well enough to translate into it.

Types of translation/interpreting:

Consecutive-interpreting individual's statement after the individual has spoken.

Simultaneous-continuous interpreting at the same time as the person is speaking.

Sight translation-reading a written document silently in one language and converting it then into another language.

Conference interpreting-interpreter at a conference in the booth using headset and mike interprets speaker or multiple speakers in various languages depending on the conference agenda and protocol.

Simultaneous-continuous interpreting during a conference

Escort interpreting-interpreting while accompanying a delegation, group or person during a plant, factory or site visit.

Sign language-for hearing-impaired/deaf

CAT-Computer-Aided Translation

Déjà Vu—translation memory computer program

NES-Non-English speaking individual

Gisting-rough draft/outline of text translation with insight into source language contents

Internationalization-designing & redesigning a product to place its localization to other countries, e.g. software applications.

Globalization-developing and manufacturing products for worldwide distribution; applicable to software, websites and publications.

Localization-adapting a product/software, websites to a specific locale, e.g., laws, languages, culture, behavior of target country.

MAT-Machine-Aided Translation.

MT-Machine Translation

MultiTerm-terminology program developed by Trados, published by SDL; a component of Trados translation memory computer program

Trados-a component of Trados translation memory computer program; see also: MultiTerm—terminology program, developed by Trados.

Bibliography and Sources

Amalrik, Andrei. *Notes of a Revolutionary, Zapiski Disidenta*. Translated by Guy Daniels. New York: Alfred Knopf, 1982.

Cracraft, James, ed. *The Soviet Union Today, An Interpretive Guide*. Expanded Edition. Chicago: The University of Chicago Press, 1983, 1988.

Dolgun, Alexander, and Patrick Watson. *Alexander Dolgun's Story: An American in the Gulag*. New York: Ballentine Books, 1976.

Epstein, Julius. *Operation Keelhaul, The Story of Forced Repatriation*. Old Greenwich: The Devin Adair Co., 1973.

Gunther, John. *Inside Russia Today*. New York: Harper & Brothers, 1957.

Laird, Roy D., and Betty A. Laird. *A Soviet Lexicon, Important Concepts, Terms and Phrases*. Lexington: D.C. Heath and Co., 1988.

Levine, Isaac Don. *The Mind of an Assassin*. New York: Greenwood Press, 1979.

Lewin, Moshe. *Lenin's Last Struggle*. New York: Random House Publishing, 1968.

Lewis, Ben. *Hammer and Tickle: A Cultural History of Communism*. New York: Pegasus Books, 2009.

Ramon Mercader, Leon Trotsky's Assassin. Signet Books, 1959.

Orwell, George. *1984*. New York: Signet Classic/Penguin Group, 1949.

Shaw, Warren and David Pryce. *World Almanac of the Soviet Union from 1905 to the Present*. New York: World Almanac Pharos Books, 1990.

Smith, Hedrick. *The Russians*. New York: Ballantine Books, 1976.

Trotsky, Leon. *The Russian Revolution*. New York: Simon & Schuster, 1959. New York: Doubleday Books, 1932.

Peter's father, Kharlampiy Kirchikov, as the soldier of the Rumanian Monarchy Army in 1940, Sibiu, Romania.

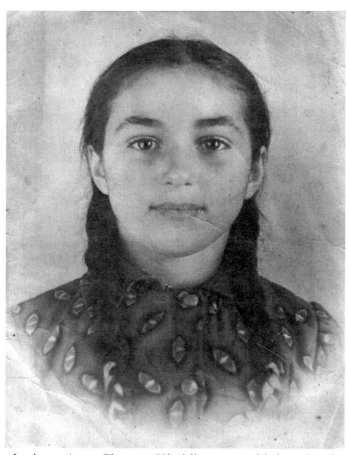

Peter's sister, Anna Chaneva Kirchikova as a third grader circa 1969
at Kirnichnoyeh middle school.

Peter Kirchikov's class of the 5th grade in 1964 at Kirnichnoyeh middle school, Bolgradsky rayon, Odessa oblast, Ukraine, USSR.

Maxim Kirchikov, Peter's son, 1987

Anna Chaneva-Kirchikova, Peter's sister, Kharlampiy Kirchikov, and Vanya Kirchikov, Peter's nephew, circa 1992

Tosh/Anthony/ Kirchikov, Ilya Kirchikov and Peter Kirchcikov, 1995

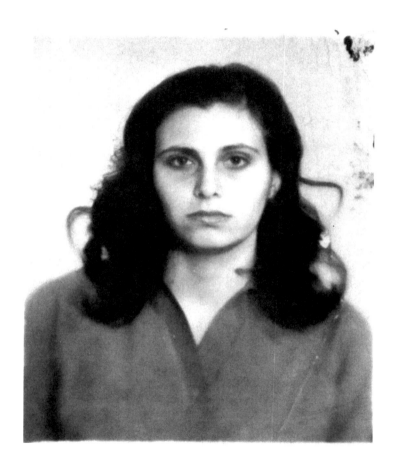

Svetlana Postalovskaya, 1991

Peter Kirchikov

Peter Kirchikov is a published writer, an approved and accredited linguist, a multilingual translator and interpreter of English, Russian Bulgarian and Ukrainian as well as other languages. He is also lexicographer, semanticist, paralegal, instructor and speaker, certified and accredited immigration court interpreter. He served as th Linguistic Quality Assurance Editor and is a regular contributing lexicographer to *Black's Law Dictionary*, the major U.S. legal authority used in the legal community worldwide and cited in courts of all levels.

Kirchikov offers multilingual translations, editing, proofreading indexing and fact-checking services. He enjoys public speaking and frequently teaches classes and seminars related to foreign languages ESL (English as a Second Language), Russian religion, literature and history, World War II, "Cold War" and Soviet eras. ***Walnuts On M Bookshelf*** is a book of memoirs about his experiences growing up in Communist Russia and his immigration to the United States. He i currently working on an *Encyclopedic Dictionary of World War I* history, operations, leaders and core terms, fragments of which hav been published on Internet and *E-Lexicon*, glossary of electronic, digita and Internet terms.

Kirchikov earned his Bachelor's Degree in English from Izmail Stat Teachers' Training College, Ukraine, USSR and his Paralegal Training Certificate from the ABA-approved National Center for Paralega Training in Atlanta, Georgia.

AWARDS AND ASSOCIATIONS

2008-Winner- Alabama Media Professionals' Communications Contest
2012-Honorable Mention-Alabama Media Professionals'
PHI BETA DELTA Honor Society for International Scholars
Alabama Media Professionals
New York Circle of Translators
Vestavia Hills Rotary Club
Bluff Park United Methodist Church

www.peterkirchikov.com